Robert Pattinson

Robert Pattinson

THE UNAUTHORIZED BIOGRAPHY

Virginia Blackburn

MICHAEL O'MARA BOOKS LIMITED

First published in Great Britain in 2009 by
Michael O'Mara Books Limited
9 Lion Yard
Tremadoc Road
London SW4 7NQ

A CIP catalogue record for this book is available from the British Library.

This book has not been approved, licensed or endorsed by
Robert Pattinson or his management.

Papers used by Michael O'Mara Books Limited are natural, recyclable
products made from wood grown in sustainable forests. The manufacturing
processes conform to the environmental regulations of the country of origin.

ISBN (hardback): 978-1-84317-404-2
ISBN (trade paperback): 978-1-84317-412-7

1 3 5 7 9 10 8 6 4 2

Designed and typeset by E-Type

Plate section designed by Joanna Wood

Printed and bound in Great Britain by Clays Ltd, St Ives plc

www.mombooks.com

contents

one love at first bite

It was 17 November 2008 and downtown Los Angeles was going wild. Thousands of people were lining the streets around the Mann Village Theater, screaming, chanting, and in some cases crying. Some had been there for hours, some had even been there for days, to witness an event that was turning out to be the show-business happening of the year. As night fell over the impressive cinema – host to some of the biggest film premieres in the world – there was a feeling of near hysteria in the air.

It was the premiere of *Twilight*. The hotly anticipated film of Stephenie Meyer's massively popular novel about a vampire and a human girl who fall in love needs no further introduction. Cars parked nearby had messages for the people the crowd had gathered to see: '*Twilight* or Bust' was written on one windscreen; 'Team Edward' was on another.

Finally, the stars arrived and the crowd gave vent to uproar: there was the snake-hipped figure they had all turned out for, one of the hottest young actors on the planet. It was Robert Pattinson, still only twenty-two, but the undisputed hero of the hour.

His portrayal of the 'good' vampire Edward Cullen in the film was one of the most fiercely debated movie performances of the decade; now fans were being driven into a frenzy by the sight of the man himself, and Robert was doing all he could to oblige. Dressed head to toe in black, the famous hair tousled and falling over his forehead, he worked the crowds like the pro he was rapidly learning to become: signing autographs, posing for pictures, hugging particularly lucky members of the throng and spreading joy wherever he went. In case there was any doubt about how the fans felt about him, one sign held up in the crowd read, 'I'm 16 years old and have never been kissed. Will U B my first?' Another, rather more prosaically, offered 'Free earplugs for RPattz' – one of the various nicknames by which he is known – if he stopped to say hello.

Robert was doing very well, coping in an atmosphere that would have had many a more experienced star heading for the safety of the theatre's interior, but even he couldn't quite comprehend the full craziness of what was going on. 'I have no other words but "bizarre",' he told reporters at MTV News, as he made his way down the red carpet. 'I left my brain at the door. It's completely insane. You never expect it – I'm completely deaf!'

Certainly, the reaction for what had initially appeared to be no more than a small, cult movie was quite beyond what Robert had experienced previously – and he had appeared in the *Harry Potter* films before now. 'This is crazier and louder than I was prepared for,' he continued to *Entertainment Weekly*. 'With every week, the fervour and anticipation seems to grow. This is my life. People know my name and ambush me in public and try to figure out what hotel I'm staying at and ask me to bite them and want to touch my hair. I have accepted it as real now, but it still feels surreal.'

It *was* surreal. Fans were so smitten that what they were doing was downright peculiar: 'There were some girls who had scratched the side of their necks, so they were freshly bleeding when they came up to get a signature,' Robert revealed. 'They were like, "We did this for you." I didn't know what to say. "Thank you, guys"?' The fan reaction surrounding Rob was certainly extreme – and sometimes dangerous. Just a month earlier, an autograph-signing session in California had gotten so out of control that one girl had her nose broken and another fainted, leading security guards to have to scrap the event.

One person who did seem to have some understanding of why the fans had gone so wild, however, was the actress Kristen Stewart, who was naturally attending the premiere with Rob and the rest of the cast, wearing an attractive one-shoulder dress with a cream-and-black top and a red skirt: the perfect *Twilight* colour palette. Kristen was Rob's co-star, playing the role of Bella Swan in the film: the ordinary American teenager who gradually realizes she's fallen in love with a vampire. In the book and the film, Edward and Bella have an extremely intense relationship, and Kristen realized that it was that – along with Robert's undeniable physical charms – that was making the fans behave in the way they did.

'The book is pretty hard core and the fans are passionate, so I understand it,' she said to reporters at *US* magazine. 'I'm looking forward to seeing the movie. Everyone is talking about it, but nobody has seen it. It's hard to talk until you see it.'

Such was the hysteria that night that even long-established A-list Hollywood icons had to struggle to make their presence felt. Jamie Foxx was seen pushing his way through the crowds so that his daughter could meet the handsome actor, while Kim Basinger and her daughter Ireland were also pictured with Rob. But then Rob was having to get used to this attention. Shortly before the film premiered, he was named by *Entertainment Weekly* as one of the Ten Breakout Stars of 2008. This was the big time – and Rob was taking centre stage.

It was the culmination of a year-long growing excitement, between him being publicly named for the part and attending the film premiere. Yet this was by no means a one-night-only affair; rather, it exemplified Rob's new way of living. Having relocated from his native England for the making of the film, and having been the focus of such a huge amount of scrutiny over the past twelve months, Rob had had to grow up fast. By this time, he had been living in a rented apartment in LA for the best part of a year, and was constantly having to cope with finding fans, now referred to as Twihards, waiting for him: 'These little teenage girls will sometimes be camped outside, but it's fine,' he was quoted as saying in *Entertainment Weekly*. 'There's something about people who like this book – they're always extraordinarily polite. If they were old men, I'd probably move.'

Now, those fans were finally getting the chance to see the film they had been waiting for. A lot hinged on the way that *Twilight* was received, not least a sequel, with all the added attention that would heap on its attractive young star. He may have had a year to get used to it – but the fact was that for Robert Pattinson, life was never going to be the same again.

It was all a far cry from a year previously. There had been great excitement when it had been announced that a film was to be made of the first of Stephenie Meyer's vampire series, *Twilight*: by means mainly of word of mouth, the books had turned from cult teen reads into a sensation, and were now selling in their millions. Meyer herself was being hailed as the new J. K. Rowling. Certainly, she had produced another series of compulsive reads with a fresh take on the supernatural. For the books' appeal was multi-faceted: not only was there the central love story between Edward and Bella, but there was this different way of portraying vampires, as creatures who could make moral choices.

In the case of the Cullens, the clan in which Edward lived, they chose to be good. These were vampires who would deny themselves human blood, slaking their terrible thirst with that of animals instead, but at a terrible cost to themselves. Ever vigilant, the vampires exercised self-control, but never lost their taste for human flesh.

Due to the books' massive popularity, there was great expectation surrounding the casting of the central figure of Edward Cullen – expectation that turned rapidly into bemusement when Rob's name was announced. 'Robert who?' seemed to be the reaction of most commentators, for although this was a young actor with a solid body of work behind him, he was far from being a household name. Indeed, the most notable element about Rob – apart from his striking appearance – was that there was a *Harry Potter* connection there, given that he'd played Cedric Diggory in the films, but otherwise, the producers were taking something of a risk. It was one that was to pay off in spectacular style.

Stephenie Meyer, however, was sure from the outset that Rob was the right choice, and it was she who announced the casting on her blog. 'I am ecstatic with [film entertainment company] Summit's choice for Edward,' she wrote. 'There are very few actors who can look both dangerous and beautiful at the same time, and even fewer who I can picture in my mind as Edward. Robert Pattinson is going to be amazing.' She was right.

For a time, however, it looked as if the producers might have made a dreadful mistake. Even from the fans who were shortly to become Rob's greatest supporters, there was a very briefly lived hostile reaction. Rob's mother felt compelled to tell Stephenie Meyer that she'd read online that her son was wretched, ugly and had the face of a gargoyle: 'I apologized to Rob for ruining his life,' said Stephenie. The canny author was, however, equally aware that this attitude was not going to last for long, and that, having had to put up with initial hostility, Rob was about to have to deal with something very different indeed: widespread adulation.

In fact, so concerned was Stephenie about the effect that this might have on him that she went to the film-makers. 'I asked the producer, "Is Rob ready for this? Have you guys prepped him? Is he ready to be the It Guy?" I don't think he really is. I don't think he sees himself that way,' she relayed in an interview with *Entertainment Weekly*.

She was certainly right about how he was soon to be perceived: within a few months, the typical online posting on the numerous message boards that were set up to discuss the film about Rob read as follows: 'When God made Robert Pattinson, He was just showing off.'

In many ways, Rob seemed just as bemused as everyone else. Given that he had previously worked as a model, he could not have been unaware that his physical appearance was not displeasing, but even so, the emphasis on Edward's looks, and by implication his own, clearly made him go a little red.

'The casting people talked to me and said, "Read the book,"' he told the website www.agirlsworld.com during an appearance at the San Diego Comic-Con, one of the numerous events that the stars of *Twilight* were required to attend in the run-up to the premiere of the film. 'I did and I just thought, "This is really dumb. It's just so pointless, even going up for it," which is what a lot of the fans said.

After I initially got cast, it was like, "He wasn't even on the shortlist." It was really left-field casting. It is kind of weird. I spent a long time thinking, "How can I take the whole beautiful thing as an interpretation?" I realized that it's just Bella saying that he's so beautiful, and she's in love with him and obsessed with him. He could be a piece of cheese and she'd say the same thing.'

Indeed, the critics might have been dumbfounded, but after that first reaction, the fans were not. From the moment Stephenie, the creator of the original Edward, gave Rob her endorsement, he turned into a heart-throb, almost literally overnight. The slightly bemused producers of another, very different film, *How to Be* – of which more later – reported a huge rise in interest in their flick as it was submitted to the Rhode Island International Film Festival: the reason, of course, was that Rob had a role (and a very different role from the brooding and romantic Edward, at that).

Edward himself was now far more than just any old romantic hero: he was to die for. He was a demi-god. He had the face of an angel, the looks of a young Greek god. He was brooding, moody, a tragic figure in some ways because he believed his vampiric status had taken away his soul, and yet capable of great passion once he'd found the right woman, which it took him the best part of a century to do. He was right up there with Heathcliff and Mr Darcy – the enduring heroes of Emily Brontë's *Wuthering Heights* and Jane Austen's *Pride and Prejudice*, respectively – in the desirability stakes and, on top of that, he was the participant in a slightly tricky love affair ... and you don't get more attractive in the eyes of female fans than that.

Rob was to talk more than once about the fact that vampires had a certain sex appeal, yet he was able to see them as piteous creatures, too; something that gave an added layer of depth to his interpretation of the role. As Rob had pointed out, Edward never wanted to be a vampire, nor chose to be one, and when, after almost 100 years of searching for a mate, he fell in love with a mortal, that carried within it potential tragedy. But he was also able to see beyond that to the innate tragedy of all vampires. Fans felt that way about it, too – it was certainly Stephenie Meyer's take on their situation – another indication that Rob understood the mentality of the people who so loved the book and the characters within.

But, although he often seemed to eclipse all others, Rob was not the only star of the show. There was also, of course, intense interest in the character of Bella, a role that had gone to the young actress Kristen Stewart. The relationship between Edward and Bella is central to the book: it was of paramount importance, therefore, that the two stars had the necessary chemistry as well. It was an issue Rob was very aware of – so much so, in fact, that his on-screen reaction to Kristen was another important element in getting him to accept the role. Indeed, the relationship between the two lead actors proved so heated that there were later to be persistent rumours that the two of them were romantically involved.

'When I was looking at the book and I thought it was impossible to play the character, I did the screen test with Kristen and I just really didn't expect the girl who was playing Bella to be like that at all,' he said to www.teenhollywood.com. 'It just drew something out. That's why I really wanted to do the movie, afterwards. It just felt really right, in the screen test. She's really, really good. She's an amazing actress. She'll be really, really big. In a lot of ways, Bella is a damsel figure in *Twilight*, but Kristen is kind of tough. It's interesting because you see this young, mortal girl having this relationship with, basically, a demi-god and she's a lot stronger, in a lot of ways, and he looks to her for support, which I really liked. Kristen really has that strength in her.'

As filming began, Rob and Kristen gave an interview to MTV News, in which they revealed tantalizing snippets about how they were playing the roles. The two were then asked about the inevitable comparison with *Harry Potter*. 'I think they're both big moneymakers ... Two big ole machines, pumping out movies,' said Kristen rather pragmatically.

Rob was more thoughtful. '[They] are using different metaphors for things,' he said. 'The strange thing about this [*Twilight*] is that it's so deeply entwined with sexuality, much more so than *Harry Potter*, as virtually all vampire things are – mainly because it's a love story. *Harry Potter* isn't really a love story, so a lot of the metaphorical stuff [in *Twilight*] is about teen lust. It's a very erotic movie.'

All of this was eagerly seized upon by the fans, who were by now desperate for any information that they could glean about their heroes and the new film. The marketing campaign was getting into gear: to whet fans' appetites still further, one of the most central scenes in the film, the fight in the ballet school in which Bella nearly loses her life, was screened on MTV.

If truth be told, the fans' reactions to the book and to Robert were now such that a marketing campaign almost seemed superfluous: as long as the film was a reasonably accurate reflection of the book, it was all but assured of massive success. And as public adoration of Robert continued to grow, the wisdom of the casting seemed ever more apparent.

In July 2008, any doubts there might have been about what a sensation the film was turning out to be were allayed by Comic-Con.

Comic-Con is a four-day convention held annually in San Diego: originally a showcase for comic books, it has expanded to include all aspects of the entertainment industry. These days, stars of forthcoming films are often scheduled to make an appearance at Comic-Con, to meet the fans – and, of course, to build up the hype.

And so, it was at this convention that the entire *Twilight* cast turned out for the first time, along with Stephenie Meyer and the film's director, Catherine Hardwicke. The crew turned up in Meeting Hall H … to be greeted by 6,500 fans. It was a mark of quite what a heart-throb Rob had become when the reaction to his appearance dwarfed that of Mark Wahlberg, Hugh Jackman and Keanu Reeves, who were also present at the convention that year.

Although the entire cast of the film was mobbed in the hall that day, there was no doubting who was the real star of the show. Quite apart from the earth-shattering reception he got when he came on stage, every time he said anything, a large portion of the audience began shrieking, 'We love you, Robert!' The questions ran along those lines as well, one particularly memorable one being, 'What's it like to portray super-hot vampires?' Another was: 'I just needed a reason to come up and talk to you, Robert.' Robert coped perfectly well, but as he was to confess, he still found it all distinctly unreal.

As the date for the premiere approached, there was some concern all was not well: it emerged on the gossip grapevine that some of the scenes in the film were having to be reshot. This was not, in the end, anything to worry about – the weather in Oregon, where they had been filming, had posed more problems than the film-makers had anticipated. In addition, due to the young age of some of those involved, some scenes had never been properly finished in the first place. That included the (hotly anticipated) bedroom kissing scene between Edward and Bella. Kristen had only been seventeen during the first takes in that scene, and so had been forced to fit in three hours of schoolwork a day while they were on set: that commitment, together with the number of camera projections needed for the shot, meant that it wasn't complete.

There was also some more work to be done on the scene in which Edward plays Bella's lullaby – focusing further on Robert's luscious, slim fingers – as the haunting melody had now finally been decided upon. In the first takes of the lullaby scene, Rob had been playing his own composition. Now that score composer Carter Burwell's tune had been selected, Rob had to reshoot the scene playing the new piece of music, so that when the camera focused on his hands, his fingerwork matched the melody.

Although Rob's composition had been cut from that scene, it emerged at Comic-Con – for the first time – that, in fact, his role in the film was not *just* to be confined to acting. Like the character he played, he was a talented musician and he was to have some input into the movie in that regard as well, with two of his pieces selected for use.

The buzz mounted: *Entertainment Weekly* ran a cover story on Robert, which, if nothing else, showed he hadn't lost his sense of humour. The cover shot had his hair taking up a fair bit of the page, fanning out in great lustrous waves … which brought him a bit of ribbing. 'I guess my hair turned into a little bit of a toupee, didn't it?' commented Robert, rather wryly, to the *Los Angeles Times*. 'I don't know what happened. I was like, it's only out for a week anyway.'

As the frenzy around the film continued to build, an interesting new angle to its mass popularity began to emerge. Robert was not the only heart-throb to come out of the movie. Taylor Lautner, the actor who plays Jacob Black, the Native American destined to end up as a werewolf in the second part of the series, was also receiving his fair share of female attention. Teen magazines were beginning to run features comparing the two idols – it didn't hurt that in the books and films they were, quite literally, deadly rivals – and there was now a Team Jacob, quite as much as there was a Team Edward.

The two actors took it pretty well, both playing up to it – 'Edward? Who's Edward? Is there an Edward character in the book?' asked Taylor in an interview with www.hollywood.com. 'I'm just kidding' – and getting on perfectly well behind the scenes. Both were aware that the book and the film were provoking some pretty extraordinary reactions; neither seemed unduly perturbed by fans who joined the other team.

Indeed, if anything, Robert was beginning to appear a little embarrassed about his pin-up status. Given the initial negative reaction when it had first been announced that he had been cast as Edward, Rob still couldn't quite appear to believe the change that had come about. 'Really, I'm a bit of a loner and not that good at dealing with other people,' he vouchsafed to the *Daily Telegraph*, adding, 'Most of the time I feel that going out is a complete waste of time. I'd rather stay in and create something than go out and talk. It's funny, but about a year ago, I'd go out and talk to girls and no one would be interested … and then when it was announced that I would be in *Twilight* and the book's author gave me her seal of approval, everyone seemed to change their mind. The attention I get now is just mind-bending.'

Rob was certainly aware that the book was the key to it all. 'It's bizarre. You kind of know that it is essentially the book. The book has so many obsessive, obsessively loyal fans,' he said in an interview with *CanMag*. 'It's strange because people just immediately relate you to the character right away, rather than you as an actor. I haven't actually looked [online] since [I got the part]. It is kind of weird. When you read the description of him, it says he's so beautiful it hurts to look at him. I think it's kind of difficult to act that so I wouldn't really know how to go about doing it. I hope there's been a lot of post-production.'

That was another sign that Rob was retaining his sense of humour – and his sense of self-deprecation, both of which were to prove crucial in keeping him grounded in the months ahead. As Stephenie Meyer had predicted, Rob had gone from 'Robert who?' to a leading heart-throb almost overnight, and many an actor who has been subject to similar adulation has gone on to lose their way. Rob has shown no signs of doing that. He has never given any indication of believing his own publicity; nor has he ever acted as if he believes he's as attractive as the fans tell him he is. That attitude bodes well for a lengthy career.

Along with the rest of the cast, Rob took part in a worldwide tour just before the film's release, provoking yet more hysteria wherever they went: 'I'm not particularly good at coping with it,' admitted Robert to the BBC's *Newsbeat*, in one of the pre-premiere interviews he was now giving to numerous newspapers, magazines and television channels across several continents.

The film was opening first in LA, and then across the world, with further premieres planned in London, Tokyo, Vancouver and Madrid, among other cities. No wonder Rob found it daunting. Yet he was surviving.

'I just cope,' he continued, speaking about the countless raucous personal appearances he had now chalked up. 'I just leave my brain at the door and just stand there. I can get the screaming more than I get the photo things. That's the worst, when you have this wall of photographers. I've never understood the logic in how they do it. Everybody shouts at the same time, and you're trying to do a logical thing, looking from the left to the right. And they almost always end up looking disappointed with you afterwards.'

That they weren't. The thousands lining the streets around the Mann Village Theater, and the millions who went on to see the film afterwards, agreed that Rob's portrayal of Edward was everything they could have asked for; the reaction was such that a sequel went into production straight away. Robert's status as a sex symbol was cemented, with the guarantee of even more attention on the horizon, something he took with very good grace.

But it was a long way from his childhood in Barnes, south London, where Robert Thomas Pattinson was born, the youngest of three siblings. So who exactly is Robert Pattinson? And how has he come to have such stratospheric success?

two a star is born

Richard and Clare Pattinson were ecstatic. The date was 13 May 1986, and Clare had just given birth to the couple's third child. In 1981, Victoria had arrived, followed by Elizabeth – known as Lizzy – in 1983, but now they had completed their family with their first boy: Robert Thomas Pattinson. They could, however, have had no idea of the glittering future that awaited their newborn son: for now, they were simply content that the boy was healthy and happy. Rob was to be the last of the Pattinsons' brood, teased and cosseted in equal measure by his two big sisters. The baby of the family, and a lively, smiley child, he was to have a perfectly normal childhood until his early teens, with no clue at all as to what was to lie ahead.

The Pattinsons came from affluent, middle-class stock. The family home – a cosy Victorian house – was in Barnes, a suburb in south-west London with the feel of a small village, although it is only a short distance by train to the heart of the metropolis. Nestling by the Thames, it has its own common, complete with pond, leading to a local nature reserve, and it is home to some of the oldest houses in London – with one road, The Terrace, hosting row upon row of Georgian homes dating from 1720. In essence, it is a quintessentially English area, characterized by affluence, tradition, a very good education system and opportunity. It is also, coincidentally, known as being home to a large acting community, of which its newest resident was destined to become a leading member.

The Pattinson family, while not actually rich, was certainly comfortably off. Richard imported vintage cars from the United States, a career his son was wryly amused by – 'My dad told me a lot of stories,' he later told the *Daily Mirror*. 'I would never buy a car from him' – while Clare worked for a modelling agency, which meant that her son was aware of the show-business world from very early on. Indeed, he was briefly to become a model himself, although strangely, given the fuss that was to be made about his looks, that aspect of his career was never a particular success.

But that was still in the future. For a rumbustious, playful and typical little boy, Barnes was the perfect environment in which to grow up: Robert and his friends were able to play on the common and in the gardens without their parents worrying overly much. Despite its proximity to the inner city of London, Barnes was a relatively crime-free environment: small children could climb trees, play games and develop friendships without constant parental supervision. It was a happy childhood, with a solid grounding, which, given the excessive reactions from fans that were to follow, gave Rob the secure background that he would need in order to be able to cope.

Nor was he treated as anything special by his siblings: in fact, as the youngest of the trio, he often had to put up with teasing and nonsense that may well account for his self-deprecation as an adult and his refusal to take himself too seriously, especially on the subject of his looks. His two older sisters could be a bit of a trial: 'Up until I was twelve, my sisters used to dress me up as a girl and call me Claudia,' he told the BBC.

This may have had its benefits – he became used to role-playing from very early on. It also revealed a certain good-naturedness about his character: far from fuming about something that might well have been mortifying at the time, Rob was able simply to laugh it off.

He certainly gave as good as he got, fighting back when his sisters became too much and letting them know they simply couldn't push him around. But above all, what stood out was what an utterly conventional early childhood he had, full of romps with the local children and all manner of childish excess. 'I remember we had a party in the garden one July,' recalled his aunt, Diana Nutley, in an interview with *Life & Style* magazine. 'We had a wonderful game to see how many doughnuts we could eat without licking our lips. It's impossible – Robert was covered in jam.'

That interview was illustrated with pictures of the young Robert. Chubby, blond and with a naughty expression, he looked the typical little boy: one to whom doughnuts and larking about were far more important than anything else – and he didn't have a care in the world.

When the pictures were published, the adult Robert, by that time an exceptionally handsome twenty-three-year-old, with a good body of work already behind him and a sensational future opening up, appeared to be very embarrassed by the images of him as a toddler. Asked to comment on them, he replied, 'Really? When I looked like a real ... weirdo?' He went on to say that the publication of such pictures should be illegal, although it would appear he was making a joke.

There was no question, though, that the embarrassment was real: most handsome young men have only to endure their baby pictures being shown by their mother to a prospective girlfriend, not hawked around to be seen by the entire world.

Rob's first school was Tower House Boys Preparatory School in East Sheen, near the family home in west London, a private, single-sex school for boys aged four to thirteen. Here he was given the first of many nicknames: Patty, a shortening of his surname. It is notable that this was the second alternative name bestowed on him that, like the first, was more commonly associated with a girl – not, it must be said, that that would have any bearing on his temperament or character. It merely illustrated the fact that, from an early age, he was getting used to the idea of taking on different personae and roles.

Rob was not an overtly academic child. A school newsletter dating from 1998 describes him thus: 'A runaway winner of last year's Form Three untidy desk award.' In other words, he was a normal, naughty school chap, who liked to play and was less keen on schoolwork. Indeed, when he went on to play the perfect schoolboy, Cedric Diggory, Prefect of Hufflepuff, in the *Harry Potter* films, Rob was keen to make the distinction between the slightly-too-good-to-be-true Cedric and himself.

Although it was not until his teens that Rob began to take acting really seriously, he was involved in school productions from a young age, beginning to join in when he was only six. Early roles included a part in an adaptation of William Golding's *Lord of the Flies*, along with taking the role of the King of Hearts in a play called *Spell For a Rhyme*, which was written by one of his teachers. He was too young to take any of it seriously, but he was good at what he did. Slowly but surely, it was becoming clear that while Rob wouldn't win any prizes for desk-tidying, or his schoolwork, the first hints of another talent altogether were beginning to emerge. Rob's teachers were starting to sense this, even if they had as yet no idea where it was all going to lead.

In November 2005, when Rob was beginning to make a name for himself as Cedric Diggory, the London *Evening Standard* newspaper tracked down the school secretary, Caroline Booth: she remembered the young Master Pattinson extremely well. 'He wasn't a particularly academic child, but he always loved drama,' she recalled. 'He was an absolutely lovely boy, everyone adored him. We have lots of lovely boys here, but he was something special. He was very pretty, beautiful and blond. I wouldn't say he was a star, but he was very keen on our drama club, I do remember that. We're all so pleased he's found something he really shines at.'

Not that it was too evident back then. The Pattinson children still had fairly standard childhoods, with family activities, holidays, and finding ways to make a bit of extra pocket money. Rob did what so many kids do: 'I started doing a paper round when I was about ten,' he told the BBC in 2005. 'I started earning £10 a week, and then I was obsessed with money until I was about fifteen.' He was joking, obviously – but it was at about that age that he was to start earning far more than his peers.

Rob's early years were ordinary in other ways, too. Like many boys his age, he enjoyed watching cartoons: 'I quite liked *Sharky & George* and then there was a cartoon with rapper MC Hammer in it – *Hammertime* – I loved that cartoon, it was genius! They don't make cartoons like that anymore,' he told the BBC. School was also unexceptional: the children would have 'school dinners. We didn't have packed lunches at my school. I was a lunch monitor as well – I used to take everyone's chips.'

When he was twelve, Rob moved to The Harrodian School, another private school in west London, set in twenty-five acres of grounds, with not only a reputation for producing good academic results, but also any number of opportunities for extra-curricular activities. With an outdoor, heated swimming pool, facilities for most types of field sports, science laboratories, a music centre and drama studios, it was the milieu of the prosperous. Harrodian was not in the same league as a school like Eton (attended by the likes of Princes William and Harry), but it was the type of place where wealthy parents – fees were £13,500 a year – sent their children for a good, all-round education, building up not only educational know-how, but a sense of confidence for the future. This was the sort of school that forms the background of British middle-class professionals: the kind of place that produces lawyers, bankers, doctors and, very occasionally, international film stars. Significantly, Rob's entrance here marked something of a turning point in his life.

For a start, unlike his earlier school, it was co-educational: there were girls all over the place. With two big sisters, Rob was used to dealing with the opposite sex, but even so, they were now all around him. He was meeting them on a daily basis, talking to them and discovering how to be friends with them. For all his slight concerns about the excesses of his fans in later years, especially the ones who want him to bite them, Rob is very relaxed in the company of women. That is a direct result of both his secure home life and his schooling, which encouraged him to be able to make friends with everyone.

Robert himself remembers it differently – 'I was a bit of a loner at school, quite anti-social,' he said to the BBC. 'My first kiss was when I was twelve, but I didn't have a girlfriend until I was eighteen.' That is not exactly how everyone else recalls it – Rob was to become a popular student with a lot of friends. The school also continued that all-important grounding that was to stand him in such good stead when he was older and his fame began to grow. And though Rob might have dismissed his teenage love life, his time at Harrodian did lead to a personal revolution of sorts. As he himself told the Beeb, he 'moved to a mixed school and then I became cool and discovered hair gel'.

He discovered something else at that age, too: modelling. Rob was still only twelve years old when he began to model. It was an industry that he had always been familiar with, due to his mother's occupation, and although this stage of his career lasted only four years, it was the beginnings of an introduction to the world he was going to inhabit.

Rob was under no illusions as to how he got the gig. 'When I first started, I was quite tall and looked like a girl, so I got lots of jobs because it was during that period when the androgynous look was cool,' he told *Closer* magazine. 'Then, I guess, I became too much of a guy, so I never got any more jobs. I had the most unsuccessful modelling career.'

It was a very astute analysis of how he'd started out, although four years as a teen model is not unsuccessful by anyone's standards and indeed, in 2007, he had another brief stint as a model, this time doing some work for Hackett. That reference to an 'unsuccessful' career is actually another indication of Rob's self-deprecation and his constant (and attractive) need never to sound as if he's bigging himself up at the expense of anyone else.

Nor has he ever entirely lost that androgynous appeal. There is something incredibly striking about his appearance, with those very sharp cheekbones, seemingly at angles to the rest of his face, which, when he was a child, could well have made him look a bit like a girl (apt, after all those years of being called Claudia and

Patty), and to this day make him stand out, head and shoulders above the crowd.

While the modelling career trundled on quietly in the background, the main focal point of Rob's life was, of course, school. And while he might have been at a cooler stage in his life, he certainly wasn't becoming any more academic. The focus of those early school reports, talking about untidy desks, had now switched to criticism of his somewhat lackadaisical approach to schoolwork – yet Rob merely maintained an endearingly sheepish attitude about his rather hopeless efforts. 'They were always pretty bad – I didn't do my homework,' he told BBC News of his school reports. 'I always turned up for lessons as I liked my teachers, but my report said I didn't try very hard.'

The fact was that, although he was never a troublemaker, Rob was simply not that interested in the academic side of his life, and he sometimes seemed incapable of buckling down to hard work (nevertheless, he did go on to achieve good exam results). Ultimately, of course, it wasn't to matter, given that he not only started to work as a model in his early teens, but moved on to become a successful actor before his adolescence was through.

When asked by the BBC who his favourite teacher was, Rob replied, 'Probably my English teacher because she got me into writing instead of just answering the question. I used to hand in homework with twenty pages of nonsense and she'd still mark it. She was a really amazing teacher.'

It was fortunate for him that it was his English teacher specifically who was prepared to do everything she could to encourage him. For another element of those early years, of which more below, was amateur dramatics. Rob now had the great advantage of not only possessing an innate acting ability but also, courtesy of that teacher, some understanding of the quality and depth of the literature with which he was to become involved. Over time, his creativity was to come out in many other ways, too, not least musically – and so this initial appreciation of the arts was to prove to stand him in extremely good stead.

Harrodian also provided plenty of opportunities for playing sports, and in this area Rob really did excel. His favourite sports are football, skiing and snowboarding, and the school encouraged all its pupils to practise plenty more besides. The emphasis was very much on turning out well-rounded individuals, physically healthy as well as academically sound, and outdoor activities were high on the agenda. They play an important role in Rob's life to this day.

Of course, the two roles that were to make his name, Cedric Diggory and Edward Cullen, were themselves both schoolboys (albeit in the first case a wizard, and in the second a vampire). This meant that there was a huge amount of interest in Robert's own school years when he came to promote the movies and discuss his roles in them.

'Was he ever bullied?' was one typical question put to him. 'No' was the answer, although even here Rob was polite, perhaps thinking that he didn't want to rub his popularity in the faces of those who *had* been bullied. Thus, as he so often did, he turned it into a joke. 'Someone stole my shoelaces once from my shoes,' he revealed. 'I still wear them and never put laces in them – they're like my trademark shoes now.'

Always a good-looking boy, it was when he was in his mid teens, mid modelling career, that Rob really began to develop the looks that would so mark him out from the rank and file. His early baby pictures show a chubby-faced little chap: now, however, the cheekbones were really starting to emerge. The almost sculpted appearance of his face was coming through. Rob has an angular look: the prominent cheekbones set off the classically structured nose and deep-set eyes. He started to stand out in any gathering, most certainly so at school.

But despite his increasingly striking appearance, he was not part of the in-crowd. 'Nope, I wasn't with the cool gang or the uncool ones,' he told the *Sunday Times Style* magazine in December 2008. 'I was transitional, in between.'

That was a good place to be. Increasingly, despite the fact that he was popular with his fellow students, liked by his teachers (even if they didn't class him as A-grade material), happy in his own skin and still nestling comfortably in the bosom of his very supportive family, Rob was developing interests outside school that were soon to dominate his life. Had he been a 'too cool for school'-type persona, he might never have taken the steps that were going to define his life. Had he been a shy geek, ditto. The fact that Rob was enjoying himself, but was neither totally in with the in-crowd nor its counterpart, meant that other opportunities were opening up. And his parents' professions helped. While on the one hand he was from a middle-class and affluent family, Rob also had a touch of the bohemian in his background: the mother who worked in the modelling industry and the father who imported not just any old cars, but vintage vehicles. Neither parent had chosen the totally conventional route and neither would he.

Now, too, there was another development in his life. Not only was Rob beginning to notice girls, girls were beginning to notice Rob. One schoolmate, Will Robinson, certainly thought so: 'Rob had a very, very big grin on his face constantly and was always cheeky in class,' he told *Life & Style*. 'Everyone liked him, though. He was a popular kid.' He was especially popular with girls. As he moved through his teenage years, Rob was developing a lanky charm, an ability to attract girls that he'd never known he had before. Long gone were the days of doughnut-eating competitions and answering to the name of Claudia: Rob was, in his own small sphere, becoming something of a heart-throb. It was as nothing compared to the adulation that he would receive a few years down the line, but it was a marked difference from his younger years. He began to realize, for the first time, that he had a real effect on women. It was not a discovery that would make him unhappy. Whole new aspects of life were beginning to open up.

Yet by no means was it just girls that were making Rob appreciate wider opportunities in life. His modelling career was still going on, and so it was inevitable that related fields would start to play a part in his mind, too. He had never forgotten those very early experiences of acting, and it would appear that, unlike the vast majority of people who try out time on a stage in early childhood and then forget all about it, something might really have stuck. Rob had a genuine talent, and it was while he was in his mid teens that this was about to blossom.

When he was fifteen, Rob really began to discover acting. He had taken part in those earlier productions, but it had never occurred to him then that this might be something he would want to pursue more seriously, still less that it would form the basis of his future career. In time-honoured fashion, it was the lure of meeting girls that made him decide to give it a go again, although in truth it was actually his father who ultimately pushed him into trying out this new sphere. Rob told the tale in typically self-deprecating fashion.

'I never did acting at [senior] school,' he told the BBC. 'I was quite shy throughout my life. My dad and I were at a restaurant and noticed this group of pretty girls nearby and for some reason decided to ask where they had just been. They mentioned the local acting school and since then he had nagged me about attending. At one point he said he would pay me, which is pretty strange – I don't know what his intentions were, but I went.'

This was, in fact, the local amateur dramatics society, the Barnes Theatre Company, and whether it was because of his early experiences acting as a young child, or simply the fact that he was a natural at it, Rob took to this new world like a duck to water. Initially he worked behind the scenes, but it wasn't long before he was taking centre stage.

'They used to do two shows a year and they are all great,' he said. 'So many people from there had become actors. Rusty and Ann, who are the directors, were actors themselves and were very talented. They were a very good group, and for some reason when I finished the backstage thing, I just decided that I should try to act. So I auditioned for *Guys and Dolls* and got a little tiny part as some Cuban dancer or something, and then in the next play I got the lead part, and then I got my agent. So I owe everything to that little club.'

The productions that Rob took part in were varied, to put it mildly: *Our Town*, *Tess of the D'Urbervilles* and *Anything Goes*. His first lead role was in *Our Town* by Thornton Wilder, something he claimed was sheer luck. 'A bunch of people left. I was the only one still there and got the position by mistake,' he told the *Daily Telegraph*. That was as maybe. Rob was making waves in a small, amateur theatrical community: it wouldn't be long before he was doing so on a much greater scale.

And that stated intention to meet a girl worked. Rob did start dating in his teens, although he has always been rather wary of revealing who the lucky girl was. By his own account, though, not only was he not really in love, he got himself very worked up about it all for no particular reason. He was enjoying dating, but he couldn't help but give in to some teenage angst.

'I remember when I was a teenager thinking my girlfriend was cheating on me, and going around riling myself up,' he said in an interview with *GQ* in April 2009. 'Pretending to cry. It was totally illegitimate – I actually didn't feel anything. I went to some pub and then went crying all the way home. And I got into my dog's bed. I was crying and holding on to the dog. I woke up in the morning, and the dog was looking at me like, "You're a fake."'

He wasn't a fake, but he was, by this time, a fully-fledged actor. Rob was getting used to inhabiting other people's personae: he was playing wildly different roles, learning to display great depths of emotion, whether he actually felt them or not, and being adept at stepping into other people's lives. Was it such a surprise that he occasionally allowed this to slip into his own life, too? If Rob wanted to play the part of the jealous lover from time to time, despite the fact that he didn't actually feel any jealousy, then that was his prerogative. In many ways, he was simply having a bit of fun. But it was acting, real acting, that was becoming his life now, and there was nothing light-hearted about that.

It was *Tess of the D'Urbervilles*, in which he played the evil Alec D'Urberville, the man responsible for poor Tess's ruin, that really got him noticed. *Tess* was Thomas Hardy's penultimate novel, first published in 1891 and now taken to be one of the greatest tales of the age. Alec is the character who initially seduces Tess, thus ruining her, destroying her later marriage to Angel Clare, and finally incurring her rage to such an extent that she murders him. It was a very strong role for such a young actor to play, and one in which Rob could give full vent to the dramatic potential of the play; indeed, Alec is in some ways a juicier role than the saintly-but-flawed Angel Clare.

His performance certainly made an impression: he was spotted by a member of the audience, ultimately resulting in him meeting and working with the international casting agent Mary Selway. For the first time, it seemed that this newfound hobby might lead to something much, much more. In fact, it was not long before his professional life would take off, of which more in the next chapter. One more amateur performance followed, as Malcolm, Prince of Scotland, in *Macbeth*, this time at the Old Sorting Office Arts Centre, also in Barnes. Shortly afterwards, the professional roles started coming in: Rob was on his way.

But there was still school to take account of. Given his decidedly haphazard attitude towards his education up until this point, it might come as something of a surprise to learn that Rob did not take advantage of these exciting opportunities by chucking it all in and making a new life for himself on the stage – far from it. Underneath the slightly scatty appearance, he was very pragmatic and having got this far with his schooling, he decided he might as well finish it. There are few more insecure professions than acting, after all, and he understood that a few qualifications would not go amiss.

However, he encountered opposition from an unexpected quarter: his father. Richard was delighted that his son was beginning to do so well, but school fees were very expensive and Rob hadn't exactly seemed to take his academic career very seriously up until now. And given that he quite clearly had a future in show business, was it really going to be worth paying for Rob to take a few more exams?

If all that were not enough, Rob was actually earning some money himself now – and rather more than in the days of that early paper round. There had been the four years of modelling, and professional acting roles were beginning to pay, too. In the end, the duo struck a compromise.

'I was at a small, private school in London,' Rob told one interviewer a few years later. 'I wasn't very academic. My dad said to me, "OK, you might as well leave, since you're not working very hard." When I told him I wanted to stay on for my A levels, he said I'd have to pay my own fees, then he'd pay me back if I got good grades.' Rob accepted the offer and got his head down.

In the event, not only did he pass the exams, but he did very well: he got an A and two Bs. This rather gave the lie to all those protestations about academic underachievement: in reality, Rob was a clever boy who could easily have gone to university if a glittering career as an actor were not now on the cards.

Nor was he just an academic achiever, either. By now it was apparent that Rob was also an extremely talented musician, playing the piano and guitar, composing his own music, and singing, of which a great deal more later in this book.

In truth, not only did Rob not look like the boy next door – being far too handsome to classify as a typical product of suburbia – but he was nothing like that average teenager either, in that he was very clever and very talented. He was, in fact, on the verge of exceptional. It's just that he managed constantly to play it down.

And that remains true to this day. Along with professing astonishment that his appearance prompts such mass hysteria, Rob is constantly self-deprecating, never takes himself seriously, never boasts, never rubs anyone's face in the fact that he's done spectacularly well at such an early age (in his early twenties, Rob is a multi-millionaire who need never work again) and all but demands to be treated like a regular guy. His co-star in the *Twilight* films, Kristen Stewart, said that he was the only contender for the role of Edward Cullen who didn't swagger on set looking utterly full of himself.

It is for these reasons, and others, that Rob is popular and liked. Above all, this approach bodes very well for the future: by taking his career seriously, but not himself, he is paving the way for a great deal more to come. And this is largely down to his secure family life and the solid grounding he got at school.

And so Rob knuckled down to his A levels, and prepared for future glory ...

three
desperately seeking success

Rob was seventeen years old, with a choice in front of him that was going to dictate the path he followed for the rest of his life. Suddenly, and slightly unexpectedly, he'd become a hard-working student, with a place at university possibly on the cards. At exactly the same time, he was up for a role in a film: as the older version of Rawdy Crawley, Becky Sharp's son, in the movie *Vanity Fair*. School or a career in film? It wasn't to be quite as straightforward a choice as it initially appeared. This was, after all, the boy who had been prepared to pay his own school fees to do his A levels. For all the insouciance, Rob was a lot more ambitious, in terms of schoolwork as well as everything else, than he usually let on.

But even so, this was quite an opportunity that had presented itself to him. When Rob started acting with the local am-dram society in Barnes, back in 2001, he had never thought that it might end up like this, with a potential career in acting ahead. It had simply been, as he so often explained, a good way to meet girls. Now, just a few years later, in 2003, he was going to act in a major movie, with one of the most famous actresses in Hollywood in the lead role.

Directed by Mira Nair, the film of *Vanity Fair* was to be a new take on William Thackeray's famous novel, although if truth be told, there were hints right from the start that this might not be one of the most successful films ever made, nor the vehicle for Rob's big breakthrough. In the end, it was to prove something of a disappointment on both those fronts, although there was great excitement when the film was first announced.

The main problem, and it was never overcome, was that the casting was a little unlikely, both in terms of the people playing the roles and their ages in relation to each other. Reese Witherspoon, who played Becky, was a somewhat surprising choice for the role: Becky is, after all, an utterly amoral creature living entirely on her wits; not an obvious association with the squeaky clean Reese. Becky was also a quintessentially English character, whereas Reese was more of a Southern belle. It had been done before, of course, an unlikely choice making a part very different from her own persona her own, not least when the American actress Renée Zellweger took on the part of the very British Bridget Jones, but even so.

Then there was the age factor: Reese was twenty-seven at the time, only a decade older than Rob, the actor playing her son in the later stages of the film. And while the make-up department could have done its bit to solve the anomaly, by ageing Reese in the course of the film, the general consensus is that it didn't. Rob looked too old and Reese looked too young. It was an early sign that this was not going to be all that the film-makers hoped it would be.

Which was a shame, for at the outset, the film looked promising. *Vanity Fair*, one of the great masterpieces of English literature, was first published in 1847–8, and follows the life of Becky Sharp, a completely amoral adventuress forced to live off her wits, as she starts the novel as a penniless orphan. She escapes the fate that had been planned for her, that of working as a governess, and instead schemes her way into high society, eventually marrying Rawdon Crawley, the younger son of Sir Pitt Crawley, who also proposes to her. The marriage eventually falls apart (though it does not end in divorce) after Becky has been discovered to be having an affair; before this, however, she bears her husband a son, from whom she becomes estranged. This was the role Rob was to play: the adult 'Rawdon Junior', in scenes staged many years after his parents had separated. Rob's film debut seemed set.

It was only a tiny part, but he was terrifically excited, all the same. It was also an introduction to the world of the film set and the paraphernalia that goes with it: 'You have a trailer and stuff,' he said some years later. 'It was the most ridiculous thing. And I was thinking, "I should be an actor. I'm doing a movie with Reese Witherspoon. How is this happening?"'

Nor was it just the luxury that appealed. Successful actors are treated totally differently from the man on the street, allowed a leeway in their behaviour that is just not open to anyone else. Unsurprisingly, that appealed to Rob too. 'It's the one job where you can go wherever you want and people have to accept it,' he said to MoviesOnline. 'If you were going to an office, got upset and said, "I need to go punch out some windows because I have to do this database," you'd be fired. But you get a lot of slack as an actor. You can just go nuts all the time.'

It was a very perceptive remark for a very young man, but Rob was right: this chance that he'd been offered meant that he'd be able to lead an extraordinary life of freedom and opportunity – if it worked out. Initially, however, it looked as if it wasn't going to.

There were quite a few setbacks in Rob's early career and one of these was what happened at the end of the filming of *Vanity Fair*. Although he was paid for the role, Rob's scenes were subsequently cut out, possibly in part because he looked more like Reese's younger brother than her son.

When the film came out the following year, in 2004, reviews were decidedly mixed. The distinguished critic Roger Ebert, writing in the *Chicago Sun-Times*, opined, 'Becky Sharp transforms herself from the impoverished orphan of an alcoholic painter into an adornment of the middle, if not the upper, reaches of the British aristocracy. *Vanity Fair* makes her a little more likeable than she was in the 1848 novel – but then I always liked Becky anyway, because she so admirably tried to obey her cynical strategies and yet so helplessly allowed herself to be misled by her heart. Reese Witherspoon reflects both of those qualities effortlessly in this new film by Mira Nair, and no wonder, for isn't there a little of Elle Woods, her character in *Legally Blonde*, at work here?'

Rather more typical, however, was this report from Cole Smithy of www.colesmithy.com: 'The first half hour of director Mira Nair's William Makepeace Thackeray-based *Vanity Fair* shows glimmers of promise before digressing into a complete and utter shambles of soft soap mediocrity,' he wrote. 'From the ostentatious costumes by designer Beatrix Aruna Pasztor to the annoying male hairstyles that permeate every scene, *Vanity Fair* is a movie that depends on its overall visual effect to hypnotize audiences into overlooking the film's plot vandalism of Thackeray's book.'

Perhaps it was just as well that Rob's contribution ended up on the cutting-room floor. The few scenes in which he appears do, however, exist on the DVD of the film, a fact that caused great relief to numerous fans about four years on, when Rob began to attain superstar status, and generated enormous interest in everything he did, and had done. It was, of course, his first ever proper acting part and, as such, has a curiosity value, if nothing else.

Despite the disappointment of not making it to the final cut (albeit a not entirely successful final cut), Rob had now had a taste of this strange new world – and he knew he liked it. This was a long way from amateur theatricals in Barnes: it was hobnobbing with the Hollywood elite in a big-name production, a world away from school, and the A levels he hadn't yet taken at this stage, and life in a London suburb.

Fortunately for him, little time elapsed before he got another chance. He was soon asked to take a role in a television production called *Ring of the Nibelungs*, which was based on the Icelandic myths that J. R. R. Tolkien had used as the basis for *The Lord of the Rings*. The classical composer Richard Wagner had also been inspired by them when writing his Ring Cycle. Rob was offered the part of Giselher, a relatively minor character compared to the roles he would soon be playing, but it was a start.

Before filming began, however, yet another chance was lined up for him by the casting agent Mary Selway, who had been behind Rob's role in *Vanity Fair* and who had no doubt been disappointed for him when his contribution had been cut. If the new job she put him up for was some sort of consolatory offering, she more than made up for the *VF* washout. For this opportunity would work out much better than any of his previous gigs – so much so, in fact, that it would go down in history as the part that made his name. This was, of course, the role of Cedric Diggory, in the film *Harry Potter and the Goblet of Fire*.

There were still a few twists and turns in the story, however. When Rob first went up for the movie, that future acclaim seemed far from assured. So it was a somewhat apprehensive Rob who approached this latest audition – and those nerves were understandable, given the high-profile nature of the job. Since the first *Harry Potter* book – *Harry Potter and the Philosopher's Stone*, or *Harry Potter and the Sorcerer's Stone* in the US – was published in 1997, the series had become a phenomenon, just as the *Twilight* series was going to do a couple of years down the line. Charting the tale of an eleven-year-old boy who lives in a cupboard under the stairs, and who suddenly discovers that he's a wizard and is sent off to Hogwarts, the wizard boarding school, the books had sold in their millions. The devotion the series had inspired among fans was so great that it was even said to have instilled a love of reading in otherwise book-averse children: quite an accomplishment in the digital age.

The films, which began to appear in 2001, had had the same cultural impact: wildly popular, they had made huge stars out of Daniel Radcliffe, who played Harry, and Rupert Grint and Emma Watson, who played Ron and Hermione, Harry's best friends, respectively. A veritable who's who of the British theatrical community had also appeared in the films: Robbie Coltrane, Ralph Fiennes, Michael Gambon, Richard Harris, Gary Oldman, Alan Rickman and Maggie Smith were just some of the names who had taken roles in *Harry Potter*. It was in these ranks that Rob could shortly belong.

It was a rather intimidating prospect. Rob had loved being on the set of *Vanity Fair*, hobnobbing with the film people and learning the ropes, but that was small beer compared to this. At the point at which Rob came on the scene, you couldn't get much bigger than *Harry Potter*, either in the book world or the film world. (Of course, a few years on, exactly the same would apply to the *Twilight* series, with Rob being the only actor to appear in both.)

Rob was up for a minor, albeit important, role: Cedric Diggory, the ultimately doomed Hogwarts student who becomes a romantic rival to Harry, among other things. Mary Selway had instantly realized that he would be perfect for the part. Cedric is decent, honourable, respectable and a thoroughly nice chap. He is also something of a heart-throb, in that Cho Chang, Harry's love interest, falls for him – a precursor of what was to come when Rob started filming *Twilight*.

And so, late in 2003, a meeting was arranged with Mike Newell, who was to direct the film: Rob, of course, was deemed ideal for the role. 'Cedric exemplifies all that you would expect the Hogwarts champion to be,' Newell told London's *Evening Standard* in 2005, when the film came out. 'Robert Pattinson was born to play the role; he's quintessentially English, with chiselled public-schoolboy good looks.'

But Rob was not to find out that he had the job straight away. Still not knowing what was going to happen to his *Potter* aspirations, Rob had to fly to South Africa immediately after that initial meeting, to start work on *Ring of the Nibelungs*, as he later explained to the *Daily Telegraph*: 'I was shooting another film in South Africa during the entire period of the casting process for *Goblet of Fire*. The casting agent had contacted my agent about seeing me for Cedric. Basically, I was able to get a meeting with Mike Newell and two of the casting directors the day before I left for South Africa to shoot this other movie. It was before anyone else had been seen for the other parts, so it was quite a cool position to be in. They did the rest of the casting for it afterwards.'

With Rob's A-level exams scheduled just a few weeks after his planned return from South Africa, packed in his suitcase on that long-haul flight were all his textbooks and revision notes. It was a very hectic time – but that busy itinerary no doubt fuelled his ambitions. The knowledge that he already had a role in *Nibelungs* when he went up for Cedric buoyed him up to such an extent that it probably factored in his landing the gig. 'I went in with this complete confidence,' he later told the *Sunday Telegraph* of his audition. 'I was convinced I had it.'

For now, though, it was a waiting game – one that Rob played with immeasurable maturity. Rob was only seventeen when he got the *Nibelungs* role and, although he was to return to the parental home in Barnes to sit his A levels, this was essentially when he began to move from being his parents' son to an independent individual in his own right. Filming in South Africa went on for the best part of four months, and he was living alone in a country he didn't know very well. It was character building. He was beginning to learn to fend for himself.

At that stage, university was still an option, but the more acting Rob did – the more he went away on location and the more he grew away from his comfortable suburban childhood – the less likely it became that he would be able to shut himself away in the confines of formal study on his return. And so it was to prove to be. Nonetheless, with the shoot taking place in the months leading up to his final exams, Rob did what he could to keep up with his schoolwork, still unsure of the path he wanted to pursue on his return.

There was genuine excitement concerning *Ring of the Nibelungs*, although it must be said that this was not going to turn into one of the greatest performances of all time. It wasn't his fault – Rob's acting was perfectly adequate and he did what was required of him. But sadly, this was to become one of those experiences shared by many a young actor: something, perhaps, that Rob would rather quietly forget. At the time, however, he was delighted finally to have a role under his belt, in which he would actually appear on-screen.

Unfortunately, as it turned out, aside from giving him the confidence to land the part that was *really* going to set him up for his major breakthrough, *Ring of the Nibelungs* was a somewhat messy affair. Written by the husband-and-wife team Diane Duane and Peter Morwood, and directed by Uli Edel, even its title is not without complications, for it is also variously known as *Dark Kingdom: The Dragon King*, *Sword of Xanten*, *Curse of the Ring* and *Die Nibelungen*. In a bizarre foreshadowing, for a time in Germany it also used the working title *Kingdom in Twilight*.

All these names were in part because it was an international production, shown in Germany, where it was well received, and Britain, where it wasn't, and in a much-abbreviated version in the United States, where the main emotion it produced in viewers appeared to be bewilderment. That is not surprising, for it had an enormously complex plot. It was also shown in Italy, Argentina and Australia: these multinational productions often end up being somewhat overblown and confusing, and this was no exception.

In brief, the story is set in the Northern European Dark Ages. Erik (Benno Fürmann), a blacksmith, who is actually, unbeknownst to himself, Prince Siegfried, goes to investigate a meteor that has hit the earth: there he meets and defeats in battle Queen Brunhild of Iceland (Kristanna Loken), the only man ever to have done so. They fall in love and promise to marry.

Siegfried then fashions a sword out of the metal contained in the meteorite and, in the company of a group of men, including the army chief Hagen, goes off to slay the dragon Fafnir, who presides over a huge haul of gold. Despite being warned that Fafnir's treasure trove is cursed, Siegfried uses it to fill the coffers of King

Gunther of Burgund (Gunther has a younger brother, Giselher, the part Rob played), keeping a ring that is part of the treasure for himself. Gunther's sister Kriemheld is very attracted to Siegfried, and uses a potion to bewitch him and, in doing so, make him betray Brunhild.

After an awful lot of further nonsense, most of the characters end up dead. This is a sample piece of dialogue from Brunhild, and it is by no means as bad as much of the rest: 'Once I loved a man, who I thought the gods themselves had sent me. I loved the whole world because he was in it. Long we were parted but I could bear it because I knew he would return one day. But when he came again it was as if his heart had been wiped clean. I loved him as I had but he did not love me. We were strangers as before we had met.'

Despite its risible script, *Ring of the Nibelungs* boasted some very big names. Alicia Witt, probably best known for playing Cybill Shepherd's daughter in the US TV sitcom *Cybill*, played Kriemhild; Julian Sands, who made his name in *A Room with a View* way back in 1985, and who has more recently played the terrorist Vladimir Bierko in the television series *24*, was Hagen; Samuel West, the highly respected British Shakespearean actor – and son of actors Timothy West and Prunella Scales – was King Gunther; and even Max von Sydow, the very famous Swedish actor (star of numerous Ingmar Bergman films and, throughout much of his life, the toast of Hollywood), ended up in the cast as a character called Eyvind, the blacksmith who brings Siegfried up. But famous actors cannot turn the mediocre into the wildly successful, and regrettably that was the case here.

Giselher, Rob's character, becomes very attached to Siegfried, and as such was a reasonably important role. He was brother to two of the main protagonists and tended to be around at significant moments: when Erik/Siegfried arrives in Burgund, it is Giselher's hawk Harmilias that lands on his arm, provoking a skirmish with some of the townspeople; it is also Giselher who tells Siegfried that his sister is desired by all but does not desire anyone in return.

He also stows away on a ship to Iceland when Gunther and Siegfried set off to visit Brunhild: by now Siegfried is under the spell and has forgotten all about the woman to whom he has pledged his love, and is planning to fight Brunhild, dressed as Gunther, so that when he overpowers her, those two can wed. It is Giselher who sees the two Gunthers and becomes suspicious, and it is Giselher who gets to find the dead Siegfried's body before trying, unsuccessfully, to avenge him. All in all, Rob got a satisfactory amount of time on-screen.

Nibelungs was certainly not your usual television fare, but it was too complicated, too hammy and too confusing to succeed. There was also the medium it was attached to – television rather than cinema – which just didn't seem to be quite the right place for such epic fare. That said, the critics were not uniformly unkind. '*Dark Kingdom* ... is not unwatchable,' wrote Charles McGrath in the *New York Times*. 'Made for about $25 million, it looks as if it cost much more, with lots of Nordic-seeming ice and mist, and a dragon that, for once, really looks like a dragon, squatty and lizardlike. The director, Uli Edel, who also made the 2001 Arthurian mini-series *Mists of Avalon*, has a feel for scenery and pageantry, and for the most part he tells the story straightforwardly, without condescending or camping it up.'

Back in the UK, the critics were not so positive. 'Forget Wagner's rousing tale of passion and magic rings, this feels more like one of those disposable pulp novels to be found lining the shelves of the bookshop's fantasy section with gaudy covers that usually feature archaic symbols, scantily clad women and the odd elf,' wrote Jamie Russell on the BBC's website. 'The dialogue's about as well written, and lead actor Fürmann is even more wooden than the Austrian Oak was when he last stepped into Conan the Barbarian's sandals. Without the pecs to guarantee respect, Fürmann's dragon's-blood-enhanced hero twirls his sword so feverishly you begin to wonder if it's a substitute for something else.'

Rob, as Giselher, is almost unrecognizable from the way he looks today. With his long, lanky hair (often in the course of Rob's career, his hair has looked as if it deserved a starring role of its own, but this was not one of those occasions), a smattering of youthful fuzz across his face that appeared as if it would never make it into a fully grown beard, and a wardrobe that seemed mainly to consist of leather jerkins, it is almost impossible to believe that Rob was shortly to become one of the most sought-after men on the planet. Nor at any point was he singled out by the critics for either his looks or his acting ability. At this stage, he was a minor actor with a minor role, and there was no indication at all that great things lay ahead.

Ironically, of course, *Ring of the Nibelungs* would probably have been completely forgotten about by this time, as yet another expensive TV mini-series that was all sound and fury conveying nothing, were it not for the fact that Rob played a small part in the proceedings. Some interest in it is thus sustained, being as it is the vehicle which provided a small role for someone who went on to become a huge star. Fans seek it out now as the earliest occasion in which Rob was seen on-screen. It crops up on dozens of fan sites, with some curiosity as to how he got involved in such an unusual project.

That was easy: it was offered him, and Rob was beginning to realize that this was the profession he might want to pursue. It was an adventure – not many boys in their late teens get to spend nearly a third of a year in South Africa, well beyond parental control. And at least it was teaching him the rudiments of his profession – just in time for a very different role. Rob's star, glowing gently as it was at the moment, was about to start shining very brightly indeed.

And he didn't have long to wait. 'The day I returned from South Africa,' he told the *Daily Telegraph*, 'I got the callback [for *Goblet of Fire*] and they told me in the audition that I had got the part.' Had it he did: it was to be a career-changing role, one that brought him worldwide fame and attention, one that was going to change his life. Rob was moving from being a nice middle-class boy from London to a player on the international film scene – it was just that no one, him included, had realized it yet.

That question about whether he wanted to continue his education had never really been answered, though, and it now became something he had to deal with. On his return to the UK, the role of Cedric was waiting for him, and Rob had to make a choice. On the one hand, he had been seriously considering studying international relations and politics at the London School of Economics, A-level results permitting; if he accepted the role of Cedric, then that aspect of his life would be completely gone, and there was still no guarantee that his participation in the *Potter* movies was going to turn him into a major star.

After all, most of the actors caught up in that franchise might have felt that they had been touched with gold dust at some stage, but the fact was that it had only made household names of Daniel Radcliffe, Rupert Grint and Emma Watson. All the other really famous names had already been famous well before they got involved. Rob was, of course, to become the biggest name of the lot of them, but back then, by choosing the notoriously unpredictable career of acting – especially over university and the chance of a settled profession – he was taking a real risk.

But the acting bug had bit. It was no longer just his amateur performances that were drawing him increasingly into this brave new world; he'd now had some experience of the real thing. He'd also sampled independence, and been out in the world on his own. But then, he had studied for those A levels ... It was a theme going round in his head: be an actor or go to university? It was a difficult choice, made easier, perhaps, by the fact that the thought of being a student didn't truly appeal to him.

Rob might have looked the scruffy teenager at this stage, but he was leading the life of an adult, now. He was earning his own money – rather more than he had done on that paper round a few years previously – and the university lifestyle did not represent escape to him in the way that it did to so many other young men. 'Even when I was seventeen, I'd go to a student bar and I'd think, "Get me out of here,"' he told the *Sunday Times Style* magazine in 2008. 'Not that I got accepted into any universities,' he added. 'Not one.'

That might have been, of course, because he knew that he really did want to become an actor and so wasn't making much of an effort at becoming a student: at any rate, now the die was cast. He was going to take the role of Cedric Diggory, and see what came of it. Rob didn't know it yet, but he had taken the decision that was going to turn him into a huge star.

That didn't mean, however, that he wasn't going to finish what he'd previously started and take his exams. On his return from South Africa, knowing that he had landed the role of Cedric, Rob had just a few weeks in which to study for his A levels, before taking them and achieving those excellent grades: an A and two Bs. His results meant that university really could have been an option: he had a choice to go on academically, whatever he might have said on other occasions about not having been offered a student place. He could easily have found one. But by this time, acting was in his blood.

Later in life, reviewers were to start concentrating on his physical appearance, and it was now, aged seventeen, that the looks and body of a young man truly began to take shape. It embarrasses Rob when he is asked about his image, and he usually manages to dodge direct questions in which he's called upon to comment on his appearance. It was thus rather ironic that when it came to the subject of his exam results, Rob appeared to be saying that yes, actually, he was just another pretty face.

For the fact that he did rather well in his A levels was dealt with in typical self-deprecatory fashion by Rob himself. 'I don't know how that happened,' he commented. 'I didn't even know half the syllabus. I lost faith in the exam system at that point.'

That remark should be taken with a pinch of salt. This was the same Rob who wanted to take his A levels so badly that he was prepared to pay to do so: under the slightly chaotic exterior was a competitive teenager who had invested two years in taking his exams, and emphatically wanted to do well. He was also managing to juggle schoolwork and what was fast turning into a full-time acting career, with not many opportunities to study, and still come out ahead on both sides. Rob was cutting an increasingly impressive figure in whatever he decided to turn his hand to.

As is clear by now, Rob is prone to behaving as if everything life throws at him is a big surprise, but underneath it all, he works very hard. Here, he made a joke out of the fact that he's actually quite clever, and distanced himself from his own personal experiences: something that was to prove very useful when he got the role of Edward, and became the focus of such intensive attention. A lesser person simply could not have coped with that. Good-looking *and* clever? Rob has never admitted to either of these qualities, but to have got to where he did by his early twenties requires a lot more than just good fortune. There's real ambition hidden under the floppy hair.

There was one small disappointment, as a potential breakthrough seemed to turn into a disaster. Rob was due to act on stage professionally, in the UK premiere of Roland Schimmelpfennig's *The Woman Before* at London's Royal Court Theatre, but he was ill and so missed rehearsals. In consequence of this, he was fired, and replaced by Tom Riley.

Happily, this was small fry compared to what was to come next. And the perceived letdown was more fortuitous in hindsight than it first appeared. Had Rob gone on to appear in *The Woman Before*, he would have become a London stage actor, known only to the cognoscenti of British theatre. Given the predilection Rob was later to show for art-house films once he'd got *Harry Potter* out of the way, there was a real chance that once on stage at the Royal Court, which is known for its independent and edgy productions, that is where he would have stayed. He'd started as a stage actor, and he might well have decided that that was where he was truly at home, with filming just a blip on the horizon. After all, his two movies to date had hardly set the world alight ...

As it was, however, he was destined to become one of the biggest film stars in the world.

four pottering into the limelight

The announcement, when it came, was greeted with, well, indifference. Casting had been completed for *Harry Potter and the Goblet of Fire*, the fourth in the series of books and films, and a little-known British actor called Robert Pattinson was to play the small but crucial role of Cedric Diggory, the handsome but tragically fated Hogwarts champion. No one was that interested. Robert who?

It was Daniel Radcliffe who was the centre of attention at that point, and given that there had been some speculation that he would not be appearing in the film, fans were immensely relieved to learn that he'd be back with the other two regulars, Rupert and Emma. Rob, like Cedric, was part of the sideshow. People were vaguely interested, but girls were still prone to shouldering their way past him to get to Daniel. He was beginning to get a taste of what it was like to be in the middle of fan-driven hysteria, but he was wading into the water gently at that point.

It has been observed before in this book, and it will come up again, that almost everything to do with Rob's involvement in *Goblet of Fire* was a forerunner for what was to happen with the *Twilight* series, but the parallels between the success of the two different series, the two women who ultimately created them, J. K. Rowling and Stephenie Meyer, and Rob's own involvement in the two remain extraordinary. For instance, this was the first time he was to assume the role of romantic hero, for Cedric was that, and more. When the film came out, it marked the beginning of a proper Robert Pattinson fan base, one that was not to reach current-day proportions until the advent of *Twilight*, but one that was to start to mark him out as a star in his own right. It's fortunate he had this early experience, too, and started to learn how to handle it; otherwise the hysteria surrounding him in later years may well have driven him mad.

Harry Potter and the Goblet of Fire, which was ultimately to become the third most successful film in the franchise at the time of writing, after *Philosopher's Stone* and *Order of the Phoenix*, was directed by Mike Newell, the first British director to take on the challenge of *Harry Potter*. He had been behind the smash comedy *Four Weddings and a Funeral* – a film which launched the career of another quintessentially English icon, Hugh Grant – and had gone on to achieve considerable success in the United States. Filming began in 2004, with a script that had to cut out huge chunks of the book, due to its length, and that now focused solely on Harry and the Goblet of Fire, rather than the vast number of additional elements that had appeared in the book.

Much of the shoot took place at Leavesdon Film Studios, just outside London, which meant that Rob could stay on his home territory for this outing. Kitted out in a school blazer with his hair slicked back, Rob certainly looked the part. He had been chosen just as much for his acting abilities as his appearance, of course, and he was perfect in the role: he managed to keep a slightly clipped quality to Cedric, as befits a public schoolboy, alongside his growing concerns about the nefarious goings-on at Hogwarts. As with the book, this film had a much darker quality to it than did the bright and breezy earlier tales – not least, of course, because Cedric was going to die at the end.

Despite the opportunities it afforded him, Rob was a little ambivalent about the role. Until that last and unexpected boost in his academic performance, he had been a reluctant student, and the thought of playing the perfect schoolboy clearly gave him pause for thought. 'I hope I'm not that close to my character. I hate him. I used to hate everybody like Cedric in my school,' was one typical remark made to the BBC around the time that the film came out; it was not to be the last time Rob was a little tactless about the work he'd done, either.

The film's bosses would not have been amused by that statement in the slightest, and it was not long before Rob had done something of an about-face, telling the *Evening Standard*, 'It's impossible to hate Cedric. He's competitive, but he's also a nice guy.'

He didn't always stick to the party line, however. On another occasion, talking to *ES* magazine, he emphasized again how different he was from the Hogwarts prefect. Asked if he'd been Diggory-esque at school, he seemed as if he could barely contain his horror: 'Not at all,' he said. 'I was never a leader and the idea of my being made head boy would have been a complete joke. I wasn't involved in much at school, and I was never picked for any of the teams.' Funnily enough, though, that was now almost becoming a source of regret. 'I wasn't at all focused at school and I didn't achieve much,' he continued. 'But I've got a sense of urgency now. I feel I can't let any more time waste away.' In actual fact, he did go on, if not to drift, exactly, in the wake of the *Potter* films, then to have a hiatus, in which he made some strange career decisions, of which more anon.

Cedric was also, like Edward, exceptionally good-looking – and not just because of the actor who played him. As noted above, there are an awful lot of parallels in Rob's participation in the two separate series, and yet another was his characters' appearance.

Both authors had made it specifically clear that, looks-wise, here was no ordinary Joe, and it was something Rob clearly felt uncomfortable about. 'This is quite difficult,' he told CBBC's *Newsround*, discussing Cedric. 'In the book, and also in my [character's] first introduction in the script, it's like, "an absurdly handsome seventeen-year-old", and it kind of puts you off a little bit, when you're trying to act, and you're [also] trying to get good angles to look good-looking and stuff. It's really stupid; you'd think I'm really egotistical. But I think that's the most daunting part about it – it's much scarier than meeting Voldemort.'

Rob was actually to appear in two *Harry Potter* films, with brief appearances in the next. Both now took the *Potter* story down a much more ominous path, and Cedric is at the heart of that action, especially in the seminal fourth instalment, *Harry Potter and the Goblet of Fire*.

The story is as follows. The threat of Lord Voldemort is back with a vengeance: just before Harry and his friends return for their fourth year at Hogwarts, Voldemort's 'Dark Mark' appears in the sky above the Quidditch World Cup Final, causing chaos, pandemonium and panic, as the magical community fears, rightly, that trouble is about to ensue.

Back at Hogwarts, the school is preparing to host the Triwizard Tournament, an international competition between three famous schools of magic: Hogwarts, Beauxbatons and Durmstrang. It is open only to the over-seventeens. Contestants, one from each school, are chosen by the Goblet of Fire: these turn out to be Cedric

Diggory, from Hogwarts; Fleur Delacour, from Beauxbatons; and Victor Krum, from Durmstrang. Then, unexpectedly, another name pops out of the Goblet – Harry's.

After a short altercation, in which Harry is wrongly accused of cheating, the contestants are set their first task: to battle a dragon and retrieve its golden egg. This Harry does successfully, but when he opens the egg to find the next clue, all he can hear is unintelligible shrieking. As a good sport, Cedric tells him to open it underwater: when he does, he is told that the merpeople have taken something of his and it can be found in the Black Lake. Breathing with the aid of Gillyweed, Harry descends deep into the lake, where he finds Ron, Hermione, Cho Chang and Fleur's sister in chains (these are all important people in the contestants' lives). Cedric saves Cho, Victor Hermoine, and Harry deals with the remaining two, since Fleur herself has not appeared.

Just before this task, however, the Yule Ball, a traditional component of the Triwizard Tournament, is held. Harry has developed a deep crush on Cho Chang and asks her to accompany him: to his disappointment, he learns that she is already being escorted to the ball by Cedric, causing something of a *froideur* between the two. Rob looks, in truth, stunningly handsome as the young romantic hero, bringing to mind nothing so much as an image of a doomed soldier, heading off to war. As a Hogwarts prefect, Cedric has a brilliant future in front of him – until he is cut off in his prime.

The third task, and Rob/Cedric's big moment, comes when the contestants must find the Triwizard Cup in the middle of a huge – and bewitched – maze. Once the Cup is found, Harry and Cedric grab the prize simultaneously, agreeing in a gentlemanly pact to be joint champions. Yet the Cup turns out to be a Portkey, a magical implement that transports anyone who touches it from one location to another. In this case, dark forces have been at work, and the Cup takes the two of them to a graveyard, where the villainous Wormtail is lurking with something that appears to be Lord Voldemort himself.

Instantly, Wormtail kills Cedric on Voldemort's command: the first key death in the *Potter* series since Harry's own parents were slaughtered. He then binds Harry to a grave and, in a scene reminiscent of voodoo magic, drops Voldemort into a burning, magical cauldron, from which he emerges fully restored. (This scene got the film rated 12: it was felt to be far too traumatic for young children.) After a duel between Voldemort and Harry, the latter manages to grab Cedric's body and then the Portkey, which takes him back to Hogwarts. After more drama, involving the teacher Mad-Eye Moody (or his 'double', at least), it is largely accepted by Harry's main allies that Voldemort is out and about again and the other two schools depart Hogwarts. The film ends, with the real fight yet to come.

Ambivalent as he might have been about identifying with his character, Rob knew what an extraordinary opportunity had been handed him on a plate. And charmingly, he was more nervous of his young co-stars than the older ones, not least because Rob himself was very much part of the *Harry Potter* generation.

He was eleven in 1997, the year the books first started to appear, and had grown up with them as the volumes were steadily released. He'd only been a few years older than that when the films first started shooting, and so he'd been charting the progress of the young stars, growing up beside them, too. When the first film appeared, Rob wouldn't have had a clue that he was going to be appearing alongside these increasingly famous teen actors, and so he found himself a little lost for words.

'I did [get star-struck] a little bit by the three main young [*Harry Potter*] guys when I first met them, it was kinda strange,' he confessed. 'We did this rehearsal week and it was kinda weird meeting these three rather iconic kids, and just talking to them normally. I couldn't really get it out of my head, "You're Harry Potter," [and] that was strange, but not really, everyone was very friendly. It's a very relaxed set.'

As already mentioned, the youthful cast were joined on set by the glitterati of Britain's theatrical community – Maggie Smith as Professor McGonagall, Michael Gambon as Albus Dumbledore, to name just two – and no doubt their presence added to this pleasant atmosphere. Rob certainly looked on these colleagues with awe, and admired their consummate professionalism.

'They make it look so easy,' he told www.virgin.net after filming had begun. 'I mean, you watch and think, "I could do that." They can do a lot of stuff in one take. Working with young people changes your attitude and they're a lot more lenient as they've been working with kids for five years. If you're an idiot they just accept it! That helped a lot.'

By Rob's own account, he was a cocky young thing when he started on the shoot, with an arrogance that had been totally taken out of him by the end. He had, after all, gone from schoolboy to actor almost overnight, and although he never really let it go to his head, by his own admission, there was a fleeting danger that it might have done.

'I've changed so much,' he told *Seven* magazine. 'I'm not nearly as cocky as I was. I was a real prat for the first month. I didn't talk to anyone. I just drank coffee and told everyone I was twenty-four and this famous theatrical actor just back from South Africa.' He was, in fact, eighteen.

This is at odds with what everyone else from that era remembered about Rob. In actual fact, he blended in with the team very well: there is always an aura of self-deprecation to his remarks and this was no different. But what did take it out of him was the sheer amount of work involved. It was to be a long shoot for a film that was teeming with special effects and needed a great deal of stunt work, of which more below, and nothing that Rob had done before could have prepared him for that.

In fact, he was so exhausted at the end of it all that he chose some very different projects to work on – projects that in some ways could have derailed his career, had *Twilight* not come along. By the time it did, of course, Rob was used to stunt work, long shoots and the sheer slog of making a blockbusting movie, and was far more able to cope with the rigours of the schedule, as he had already learned the ropes on *Harry Potter*. Without Cedric, there would have been no Edward – or not the way that Rob played him, at least. But it was a sharp learning curve and Rob had to learn a lot, fast.

When the *Potter* film opened in 2005, Rob came in for a lot of scrutiny. It was as nothing compared to what he was going to experience as Edward Cullen, naturally, but it was a sort of dry run for what would be happening a few years hence. Cho Chang wasn't the only girl who clocked the handsome Cedric's charms: quite a lot of other girls did, too, and for the first time Rob started to have a fan club of his own. It did not develop into the hysteria of later years, but girls were clearly dividing into Harry fans and Cedric fans, and there were more of the latter than you might think.

After all, Cedric was briefly almost as high profile a role as Harry, in that he was at the forefront of the promotional campaign for the film – which, let's not forget, was a global affair. The poster advertising the movie had the central trio of Harry, Ron and Hermione in the foreground, but Cedric was just behind them, preparing to take part in the Triwizard Tournament. He also appears on the cover of the DVD; while in the run-up to the film's premiere, he featured heavily in the stills that were released to the press, not least in the rivalry he has with Harry. But 'briefly' is the key word here. Cedric is one of the first characters to die in the books, something that niggled slightly with Rob. 'I looked at the other actors and thought, "Lucky you! You've got another three films guaranteed!"' he told *ES* magazine.

In the event, *he* was lucky. Had he, too, had another three films, he might not have been available for the role of Edward, which pitted him into the stratosphere, to cultivate a fan base that was even to outstrip that of Daniel Radcliffe himself.

And anyway, there was a certain kudos about being a high-profile *Potter*-related death. 'The cemetery scene was the bit I was most looking forward to doing,' Rob said on another occasion. 'No one has died in it so it's always going to be the first death in *Harry Potter*. It was cool, one of the best parts of the part, I think.'

As for the on-screen chemistry between him and Cho, played by Katie Leung, it was there, but not in quite the same way as it was when Rob met Kristen. There had been no screen test here to assess the vibes flying between the couple, for a start, but then the relationship between the two was not central to the story. The pair were friendly, and the scenes between them unforced. 'I get on really well with Katie, she's a really cool girl,' said Rob to CBBC's *Newsround*. 'I dance with her and there's lots of scenes [involving] holding hands and stuff like that.'

Naturally, it was nothing like as intense an on-screen relationship as he was to go on to have with Kristen – but then these characters were a little younger than Edward and Bella. And Cedric didn't have quite the fiery passion that Edward did in his blood.

Sounding very much more tactful than he had done previously, Rob was asked what he had in common with Cedric. ('Not a lot' was the real answer, but he knew better than to say that by now.) 'I sort of identify with him in a couple of ways,' he continued to *Newsround*. 'I am not as nice as he is; he tends to do the right thing all the time and I never need to do that. I generally am quite pleasant. I think he is too, and that's one of the basic similarities. Let's see, I've got blond hair, I don't know, and I am relatively sporty. I think he is a better person than me.'

Naturally, there was a great deal of curiosity about filming, especially the Triwizard Tournament maze scene. Rob was asked if it had been difficult to film. 'Yeah, that whole sequence was pretty intense,' he commented to *Newsround*. 'They shot it right at the beginning – within my first week I shot in the maze. It was really difficult to translate all the things in the book that happened in the maze – like all these riddles and things – into film. It was almost impossible. The way Mike Newell did it was really good. He came up with the idea that in the maze it is just the fear and the darkness and the isolation that kind of drives all the competitors a bit insane. We were really hyped up.'

It shouldn't be forgotten that this was all still extremely new to Rob. Despite the massively high profile of the project, and the importance to the story of the part he was playing, this was still only Rob's third professional role on film. It is a mark of how much the director trusted that he could pull it off – and indeed, how fast Rob himself had to come to terms with the ins and outs of filming – that he managed to succeed in the role in the way he did.

'You are on one-hundred-per-cent adrenalin and you're starting this in the first week and you have just met all the other actors the week before and now you have to go crazy with them,' Rob continued, recalling those first few weeks. 'That was pretty intense, but I think it was really the most fun, because it was really physical work. Shooting wands at each other was really fun. The swimming thing was pretty physical too. In fact all my scenes were kind of action scenes. They were all pretty physical.'

The swimming scenes were undoubtedly a challenge, in that they were actually shot underwater, in a sixty-foot-deep, blue-screen tank. Rob had to learn to scuba-dive to perform in them, another indication of what a challenge the role was turning out to be.

'Yeah, it was really strange,' Rob went on. 'It is completely blue in there and there are divers with breathing equipment that are completely blue as well. You can't really see anything. You just get this breather put into your mouth after the take has been done. We would do a thirty-second take and I couldn't let bubbles come out of my mouth or anything because I am supposed to be able to breathe underwater in the movie. It was strange to be underwater. You don't feel so self-conscious at all; it is a nice thing. You can't see the crew. You can't hear anything. It is really nice, but you can't breathe.'

This is clearly where his sporting prowess came to the fore. As Rob himself had pointed out, about the only thing that he and Cedric had in common was that they were both keen on physical activity, and so even though Rob had had to learn to dive in order to film the scene, he was not put off by anything it involved.

Asked if it was scary, he responded, 'Not really. I had never done scuba-diving before, so I did training during the first week. I was in a tiny little tub that was a practice tank. I did not see the big tank until they first started shooting in it. It was about a hundred times the size of the practice tank and it was so much deeper, so that was sort of scary when I first got there, because you have to get used to all the pressure and things like that. I don't know if you have been scuba-diving, but it is very different. I thought it was really easy in that little shallow pool, because it is, but when you are doing it in a really deep tank it is kind of scary at first. I got used to it quickly though.'

Rob's natural modesty and good humour stood him in good stead in other ways, too. The film contained quite a bit of material about teen rivalry, specifically between Harry and Ron, as Ron starts to believe that Harry is deliberately trying to make himself the focus of everyone's attention and consequently gets very jealous indeed. In addition to that plot line, Harry has a crush on Cho, who, in the time-honoured manner of love triangles, goes on to fall for Cedric, as related above. Somewhat appropriately, there was the chance for off-screen rivalry, too.

Ever since the inception of the *Harry Potter* films, Daniel Radcliffe had been very much the star of the show. Even when he started, aged eleven, he got his fair share of attention from besotted *Harry Potter* fans, and, as he was growing older, he was becoming a bona fide idol. This status included, of course, the adoration of young girls, who thought of him as their ideal man. Until the fourth film, none of the other young stars of the franchise had ever provided a real threat.

Rob was a different case altogether. With those heart-stopping looks, no longer played down as they had been in *Ring of the Nibelungs* – indeed, he was buffed up to perfection as the ideal schoolboy – he was beginning to attract some serious attention as a lust object. This could have had the effect of putting Daniel's nose out of joint, which could have made for unpleasantness on set had Rob been minded to wind him up. Instead, and very charmingly, he did exactly the opposite.

'I think, in real life, [Daniel's] just so far superior to me in terms of desirability, he didn't really have much of a competition with me,' Rob told CBBC's *Newsround*, in response to a question about whether they teased each other on the grounds that in the book they weren't supposed to get on. 'So there wasn't really much joking around. I'd probably cry if he did. If I was Katie, I would definitely go out with him, because he's rich and famous, and I'm not, really.' It was not necessarily a view his growing army of fans would have agreed with, but it certainly kept matters calm.

All the work – difficult stunts and all – proved to be worth it in the end: the film went on to garner spectacular reviews. 'It's refreshing that *Potter 4* aspires to be a paranoid thriller, rather than yet another detective mystery,' wrote Angie Errigo in *Empire* magazine. 'House points, too, for the movie's terrific effects and considerable charm.'

'As a spectacle, *Goblet* is deliciously dark, wickedly funny and superbly mounted; it also sports some fine turns, especially Ralph Fiennes's evil Lord Voldemort and Brendan Gleeson's cock-eyed wizard, Alastor Moody,' said *Time Out*. 'Newell keeps the action centred on two key events from the book: the Hogwarts Yule Ball and the Triwizard Tournament (a distinctly dangerous trio of tasks involving stupendously rendered CGI dragons, scary mermaid-like octopuses called Grindylows, and an ominous maze).'

'Let the adjectives roll: this is the most thrilling, exciting, magical kids' movie I've seen since, well, the last *Harry Potter* film' was David Edwards's view in the *Daily Mirror*.

Mike Newell's 'considerable triumph is to keep the thrills up to exhilarating scratch', opined James Christopher in *The Times*. 'One of the perennial joys of J. K. Rowling's addictive series is the ability to generate ever spookier shades of evil. Here, the fear comes in the form of scary dragons, a poisonous vision of Lord Voldemort. Ralph Fiennes's wispy ghost is an ice age chillier than previous incumbents.'

The audience agreed. *Harry Potter and the Goblet of Fire* racked up countless impressive records: less than a week after its release, the film had taken over $102 million at the North American box office, which was the biggest first weekend gross for any *Harry Potter* film. In total, it earned over $895 million globally, which put it in the number-one slot of high-grossing films of 2005, and made it the eighth highest-grossing film of all time. It became the only *Potter* film to win a BAFTA, for Best Production Design, and it was also nominated for an Oscar for Best Art Direction, in the event losing to *Memoirs of a Geisha*. In short, it was a staggering success.

And so it went on. The reviewers were, on the whole, positive about everyone involved: the regular cast, the newcomers (especially Fiennes), the director – everyone. But the person who really stood out to reviewers, who knew a hot young star when they saw one, was the actor playing Harry's love rival. As some of them put it, Rob didn't just steal the show – he got the girl, too.

But Rob's new status was not yet totally assured, as he related himself in a good-humoured anecdote. 'At a premiere for *Harry Potter*, all these people were screaming, and this girl asked me to sign something,' he recalled to *Glamour* magazine. 'Halfway through, Daniel Radcliffe came along and the girl snatched the pad away, saying, "I want Daniel!" So I just shuffled off.'

But that was not to last for long. Rob had known that taking part in such a high-profile series was bound to get him noticed, and so it proved. Aged just nineteen, he was on the cusp of stardom, although the attention he provoked in the role of Cedric was but a drop in the ocean compared to what was going to happen when Edward came on the scene. 'Someone asked me for my autograph the other day, which is quite cool,' he told CBBC's *Newsround*, in an interview just after the film came out, which reads now like a charming period piece, given what was about to happen to him in terms of popularity. 'But I don't know. I hope it [*Potter* mania] doesn't make me not come out of my house, because I barely come out of my house as it is.'

And that is the other clue to Rob's character, and one of the reasons he was to play Edward so well: he was not always gregarious. While not exactly a recluse – he had a couple of very close friends he hung out with, including fellow actor Tom Sturridge – nor was he Mr Partytime. One of the notable facets of Rob's acting is that he often manages to convey the sense of being an outsider, something that was utterly crucial to the role of Edward. And, of course, that slight aloofness only increased his desirability. There is always a sense, even when he is at his most humorous and self-deprecating, that he is holding something of himself back. Rob has never given the impression of being overly eager to please, and this, too, has played a large part in his charm.

The final element of the dry run that the *Potter* films were providing for the *Twilight* series came at the premiere. Rob had turned nineteen by the time the film was released, on 18 November 2005, and although the lion's share of attention still went to the three central stars, there was no shadow of a doubt that a new star had been born. 'I was actually having nightmares about it for months in advance,' said Rob in an interview with the *Daily Telegraph*. He went, he said, to Jasper Conran and chose 'the most ridiculous, extravagant clothes – they looked really good in the shop. And then I put them on and I thought: "You look such an idiot."'

At the premiere itself, in fact, Rob looked like nothing so much as a rock star, sporting black leather trousers, a white cotton shirt billowing out of them, and a dark red velvet jacket. One observer commented that he could have been Mick Jagger's prettier younger brother. Towering above his co-stars, Rob is pictured with arms around Rupert and Emma: although they were the bigger names back then, looking at the photos today there is no doubt who is destined to be the huge star. Without even meaning to, Rob was standing out from the rest.

There were 12,000 people in Leicester Square that day, and a fair number wanted to see Rob, the new kid on the block – and the next big thing. 'I was in a trance the whole way through it,' he remembered. 'The day before I was just sitting in Leicester Square, happily being ignored by everyone. Then suddenly strangers are screaming your name. Amazing.'

Rob was beginning to attract serious notice, with *The Times* naming him as one of the People of the Year under the headline 'Almost Famous'. 'This fresh-faced, photogenic nineteen-year-old so oozes charm and likeability that casting directors are predicting a big future,' wrote Patricia Dobson, the compiler of *Screen International*'s list of British stars of tomorrow, which was used as the foundation of the *Times* article. Dobson continued, 'Despite his initiation via *Harry Potter*, Pattinson cites Tim Burton and Todd Solondz as directors he admires for "breaking boundaries".' As it was to prove, those choices were also an indication that Rob wanted to break some boundaries of his own.

A star was born – almost. Rob had been launched into the world on the back of one of the most high-profile and successful film franchises ever made. But it was going to take him a while to build on that success, and to take the step into the *really* big time, because, for the present, he drifted. He made some very strange decisions about what he wanted to do next. He took some time off, while not doing anything at all.

It had all happened so quickly – that leap from Barnes amateur dramatics to an appearance in the *Harry Potter* franchise – that Rob appeared stunned by it all. With something of the lone wolf about him at the best of times, he retreated into himself. On the brink of massive success, Rob was in danger of throwing it all away.

five bad hair daze

With the first *Harry Potter* film in the bag, the world should have been Rob's oyster. Anyone who took part in that particular film franchise was guaranteed a worldwide audience of hundreds of millions, and a near-guarantee of further, massive, success. And that should have been more true for Rob than most. *The Times* had already pointed out that his star was in the ascendant; now *Teen People* magazine did likewise and named Rob 'the next Jude Law', the first of a number of such comparisons between Rob and the older actor.

There was a faint facial similarity between them (although Rob had the edge), but it was a comparison that frequently embarrassed him. There could have been many reasons for that. To begin with, most actors don't like being compared to other actors, as they prefer to feel they are the one and only Robert Pattinson, not the next someone else. (Stephenie Meyer was to have the same experience, in that she was repeatedly called the next J. K. Rowling, of which more anon.) Secondly, although Rob would never have said this and probably never consciously thought it, after his early days as an actor and New Big Thing, Jude Law's reputation had become rather tarnished.

His personal life appeared sleazy in the wake of a slew of

revelations about affairs with nannies and the like, while his professional reputation had suffered, too, in that his career was no longer quite as hot as it had been. To be compared to Jude Law was not the unalloyed delight it might once have been. And anyway, Law had a receding hairline. Rob's hair was his pride and joy.

But he wasn't doing a great deal. For a start, as he put it, he spent some time hanging around LA with a group of waitresses; any time he did bestir himself, it was to go to meetings. Rob loved meetings.

'I like meetings there [in LA] a lot,' he told *Seven* magazine. 'You go in, no one cares if you're a nice person or not. You just do it and if you can do it, you do it, and if you can't, you can't.' That was as good a summary of the film industry as anyone has ever made. But those meetings were not resulting in anything, in part because Rob was just enjoying himself as he was, hanging out in the sun and having a nice time. Money wasn't a problem: he'd been earning his own money for a while now, and in the wake of the *Potter* extravaganza had enough to get by.

Even so, Rob was having to learn how to behave in very different situations. His childhood had not exactly been a sheltered one, but many a young British star has gone to Hollywood, there to fail, or at least to make an idiot of themselves by simply not understanding the way it all worked. Rob did not fall into that trap. He was just old enough to start enjoying pub culture in London, but he appreciated very quickly that it did not travel overseas, as he told *Seven*. 'In England, if you want to look rough,' he explained, 'you go out and get really drunk and come in looking really hungover, but if you do that in America, it's like, "Have you got a drinking problem?"' It was wise to cotton on so fast: Rob was to be spending a great deal of time stateside, in the future.

It was becoming increasingly apparent that he was not merely standing out from the thousands of other aspiring actors for his exceptional appearance alone: here was a *really* talented actor, capable of taking on hugely different roles and making them his own. His role as Cedric Diggory might not have been as big as that of Harry and his close friends, but it was central to the story of *Goblet of Fire*, and it was widely accepted that Rob had carried it off brilliantly. This, therefore, should have been his time.

But it wasn't. Rob was often to emphasize to interviewers, and to anyone else who asked, that he almost fell into acting by accident. And perhaps it was that lack of a game plan which led him to make a few career choices that were not quite what one would have expected. For a start, he worked on a few projects for television, rather than appearing in another blockbuster, à la the *Potter* series, and secondly, at least one of these projects was decidedly beneath him.

Nevertheless, he was still very young, just starting out in the industry, and so perhaps it should be no surprise that it took him a while to make the next big step. Indeed, at this stage, it wasn't entirely clear that Rob would stick to an acting career. After all, it had never been his burning ambition, and even until he finally signed on to play Edward, he was still contemplating giving it all up.

After a short time of getting nowhere in LA, Rob returned to the UK, and found a tiny little flat for himself in the middle of London, in Soho, long the haunt of bohemian types. Soho is a beguiling area: once the red-light district of the capital, these days it is home to small-scale production companies, magazines, some excellent restaurants and any number of artists and their hangers-on.

Almost villagey in its atmosphere, despite the fact that it is at the heart of the metropolis, Soho is the kind of place where everyone knew each other. One could regularly bump into acquaintances on the narrow streets and in the local bars and cafes. It was the perfect place for a young man to hang out.

'It was so cool,' Rob later recalled of that time. 'You had to walk through a restaurant kitchen to get up to the roofs but you could like walk along all the roofs . . . I didn't do anything for a year, I just sat on the roof and played music . . . it was like the best time I had ever had.'

It was around this period that Rob got together with the model Nina Schubert. They did not know each other from showbiz circles: rather they lived round the corner from each other in London and knew each other from the old days in Barnes. They parted on very amicable terms, with Nina ultimately moving to New Zealand to pursue a career as an artist.

Rob and Nina mixed with a like-minded set of young people starting out in show business. Nina, tall, blonde and shapely, travelled the world as much as Rob did, having worked as a model for six years after she was spotted at the age of seventeen.

'I was seen by an agency in Covent Garden, walking round the streets with my friend,' she told the website www.stuff.co.nz. 'I had a look that someone noticed. I was in a film when I was seventeen. It was called *Dream*. There are gaps in the market and you never do it constantly. I travelled everywhere many times: Milan, London, Paris, Spain, New York, Mexico; fashion mag and catalogue shoots and catwalk shows. I enjoyed the fact that I travelled, but the majority of the time it was tedious work. You spend a long time waiting around. But it's very well paid.'

The relationship ended in 2006, but the couple stayed friends.

Nina went off to live in various global locations before settling in Hawera, New Zealand, where she was getting on with her life until suddenly her ex-boyfriend became the hottest property on the planet and interest in her soared. Neither she nor Rob has ever spoken in any detail about the relationship, but she did confirm they were friends.

'Rob is still a really good friend of mine,' she told the website. 'He's hopefully going to come here, if he can get a break from working. I gave him my paintings when we lived together in London. Now he's commissioned me to paint one for him and I'm working on it.'

Back then, living in London, Rob spent a lot of time hanging out with Nina and his friend Tom Sturridge; if anything, music was his focus, far more than acting. But if he didn't start making proper plans and find the next big project to work on, his new career would fade, and he was coming to realize that he didn't want that to happen. So, he began to think about what to do next.

Rob's choices at this juncture were not what you would expect from a newly discovered star of one of the most successful film franchises of all time. He could have had his pick of teen roles at that time, but he didn't want them (ironically, given that Edward Cullen, at seventeen, is the ultimate teen role), and instead signed up for some fairly small-scale projects, quite different from any other roles he had played to date. It seemed as if he was testing what was open to him and what he'd be able to take on that he hadn't done before. This might also have had something to do with the people he looked up to.

Rob's hero when it came to acting couldn't have been more different from Rob himself. 'I aspire to be Jack Nicholson,' Rob told an interviewer. 'I love his every single mannerism. I used to try and be him in virtually everything I did, I don't know why. I watched *One Flew Over the Cuckoo's Nest* when I was about thirteen, and I dressed like him. I tried to do his accent. I did everything like him. I think it kind of stuck with me.'

Many people have found Rob's choice of Jack Nicholson as an actor to aspire to surprising; latterly, Nicholson does not cut as appealing a figure as he once did. But in his younger days, not only was he a strikingly handsome man, but he was also a ground-breaking actor. His performance in *One Flew Over the Cuckoo's Nest* has gone down in cinematic history as one of the all-time greatest screen performances, while later roles in films like *The Shining* and *The Witches of Eastwick* ensured that he stayed at the top of his game. Despite the sometimes lurid headlines he's occasionally garnered, Nicholson is very much an actor's actor, and in idolizing him, Rob sent out a clear message that he was taking his profession very seriously. He didn't want to be just a heart-throb: he wanted to act.

Nicholson could not have been more disparate from Rob, both privately and as an actor, but he was known to take risks when he was a younger man, and that might have been what prompted Rob to take a few risks of his own. With Rob having just starred as a classic teen hero, everyone expected him to play another public schoolboy, possibly one fighting the forces of evil, and so he turned the tables on everyone, and chose a very different route.

Rob's first choice was, actually, understandable from an acting point of view, for it certainly stretched his range. He took part in a television film, made to be shown on BBC4, that was so different from the *Potter* outing that it might have been seen as a deliberate early attempt to escape being typecast as yet another teen idol. The film was called *The Haunted Airman*, and although not many people appeared to notice it when it went out, the few who did so gave it – and Rob – exceptionally good reviews.

The Haunted Airman was based on a Dennis Wheatley novel called *The Haunting of Toby Jugg*, and adapted by Chris Durlacher. Rob played Toby, an RAF bomber pilot who has been traumatized by his participation in the bombing of the German city of Dresden towards the end of the Second World War, and is also paralyzed from the waist down. He is sent to a remote mansion in Wales to recover, where he is looked after by the sinister psychiatrist Hal Burns (Julian Sands, with whom Rob had previously worked on the *Nibelungs* film). After a fairly short period, Toby begins to suffer from nightmares and hallucinations, in which blurry figures and insects crawl across his consciousness and, indeed, his person, it being unclear whether these have been brought on by the guilt he felt in taking part in the bombing raids, or his treatment by Dr Burns.

Into this increasingly nightmarish picture steps the figure of his aunt Julia, played by Rachael Stirling, with whom Toby is infatuated, but who appears to be involved with Dr Burns. Toby has been sending letters to her, describing his anguish, which have, of course, been intercepted by the doctor. Toby believes that his psychiatrist has been spying on him: soon he begins to think that his aunt is implicated, too.

There was a strange, creepy, almost gothic horror feel about the film, which nonetheless scored a very high critical rating. On www. britmovie.co.uk, it is described as follows: 'This film largely eschews obvious scare tactics and supernatural Hammer hokum, but relies on mood and creepy camerawork to suggest a sense of psychological disarray – which also means it's almost too intelligently understated for its own good.'

It was a good point, but Rob had been seeking something low-key. He had made no secret of the fact that the *Potter* experience could at times be overwhelming: a high-brow tale on a minority channel made the perfect contrast, the only problem being that no one had watched what he had done.

Nevertheless, his performance continued to impress those in the know. Previewing *The Haunted Airman* in *The Observer*, Sarah Hughes observed, 'BBC4 pulls the stops out for Halloween with this spooky adaptation of Dennis Wheatley's 1948 novel *The Haunting of Toby Jugg*. Robert Pattinson (probably best known as Cedric Diggory in the *Harry Potter* films) gives an astonishingly good performance as the eponymous Toby, a crippled airman tormented by both war flashbacks and remorse. His sinister doctor Hal (a suitably menacing Julian Sands) attempts to get to the bottom of Jugg's guilt and to his relationship with his aunt Julia (Rachael Stirling). This is a sombre, chilly and utterly absorbing adaptation, but two words of warning: fans of the novel should note there are differences to the plot, and arachnophobes should probably steer clear altogether.'

That was something else Rob was learning to endure for his art. All manner of creepy-crawlies appeared in the film, as often as not crawling across him. But that aside, the experience taught him more – and more importantly – about how to create a very dark atmosphere using subtle techniques, which were sure to be invaluable in the years to come.

Rob was still a little ambivalent about whether he wanted to stay in acting, but on the days when he *was* certain that it was his chosen career, he was beginning to think in very ambitious terms indeed. The idea of running his own production company was beginning to form and so working on a project such as *The Haunted*

Airman was going to prove very useful for that, as the small, low-budget production had taught him that, given the right artistic vision and clever techniques, something rather special could be created. As long as a venture had integrity and skill, anything could be achieved.

Critic Harry Venning also observed the nightmarish quality of the film – as well as the physical attributes of its lead actor. 'All the BBC's blue filters [lighting gels] must have been requisitioned for *The Haunted Airman*, a very disturbing, beautifully made and satisfyingly chilling ghost story,' he wrote on TheStage.co.uk. 'Set in a convalescence home for shell-shocked servicemen during World War Two, it starred Robert Pattinson as a wheelchair-bound RAF pilot suffering from trauma, guilt and paranoia.

'Either that, or he's actually imprisoned in a private hell run by the devil himself, who sends spiders, birds and the spirits of the dead to torment him. Make up your own mind. Pattinson – an actor whose jawline is so finely chiselled it could split granite – played the airman of the title with a perfect combination of youthful terror and world-weary cynicism. Julian Sands provided creepy support as the oleaginous Dr Burns, with Rachael Stirling as the airman's solicitous and attentive "aunt".'

A review in *The Independent on Sunday* also made much of that jawline, although it was not quite as complimentary overall, as the majority of other critiques had been: 'I enjoyed the slightly amateur feel to this year's Halloween scheduling. *The Haunted Airman*, on BBC4, was achingly overlong, but occasionally a nasty spider and spooky sound effects were deployed to keep your interest. It was just saved from inadequacy by the bone structure of the airman (Robert Pattinson). He was playing a character called Toby Jugg, but he sure didn't look like one. Like Catherine

Deneuve in *Repulsion*, he was so beautiful that you kept watching, spellbound, even as he made a really rather slow and predictable descent into psychosis.'

In all, Rob had acquitted himself exceptionally well, the only problem being that viewers of the film were few and far between. The channel on which it was shown, BBC4, was a digital channel, not one of the mainstream viewing outlets: and at the time, in 2006, it did not have mass appeal. Rob was certainly beginning to prove that he was an actor to be taken seriously – and was not just a one-trick pony with cheekbones that could slice bread – but even so, what was the good of being a truly awe-inspiring actor if no one actually saw him act?

Indeed, at this stage, Rob had only really scored one major success in box office and profile terms – all-important if you want to make it big on the silver screen – and that was in *Harry Potter*. His scenes in *Vanity Fair* had been cut out and the *Nibelungs* saga was best forgotten. There really was no sign at this point that Rob's career was about to take off. He is often written about as if he stepped straight from *Potter* to *Twilight*, barely pausing for breath, and yet there were actually a few years in the middle of it all when his success was very far from being assured.

Still, he was happy in his own life. His parents were only a few miles away in Barnes, he had friends, he had his music, and Rob was enjoying the life of a young man in a huge city, with all the potential for enjoyment that was there. He didn't feel under a great deal of pressure to do anything much at that point, although his leap into superstardom was coming increasingly near.

But it certainly hadn't come yet. His next project, frankly, was an appalling choice. Although on paper it must have looked good at the time, combining as it did various social issues, including teenage pregnancy, dealing with Alzheimer's, searching for identity and family tension, this could have been a serious setback in Rob's career, if people in the know had consequently viewed him as an actor who had flowered so briefly in the role of Cedric Diggory, but was now reduced to appearing in dross. As it happened, his career wasn't affected, but it gave him a salutary taste of what it is like to play a role in an absolute stinker – and this time round, even his own performance came in for some stick.

The Bad Mother's Handbook, based on a novel by Kate Long and directed by Robin Sheppard, was a drama made for ITV. Karen Cooper (Catherine Tate), having had a child when she was still a teenager, is fed up with her lot. To make matters worse, she discovers that a) she is adopted, and b) her seventeen-year-old daughter Charlotte (Holly Grainger) has been dumped by her boyfriend. The daughter is also pregnant, leading Karen to fear that history is repeating itself and that her daughter will also be placed on the path to an unsatisfactory life.

Meanwhile, Nan (Anne Reid) has Alzheimer's, something that Karen must deal with, along with trying to find her birth mother. Charlie, as the daughter is known, is feeling alienated from the other two women in the family, and starts to lean on her new friend Daniel (Rob). Daniel is what we would politely term 'socially awkward', and less politely, a geek: Rob is almost unrecognizable with lank hair, especially tamed for the occasion, and spectacles, acting as a person who is quite remarkably uncool.

If he hadn't been much like the character of Cedric, then he was even less like the character of Daniel, and it is difficult to know what possessed him to take on the part. Then again, you could have said that of anyone involved in the project, for it simply turned out to be one of those ventures that went totally wrong.

The plot is actually far longer and more convoluted than described here, at times barely believable. At least you could say this, though. He got the girl in the end.

Most of the attention garnered by this offering focused on Catherine Tate, a comedienne then best known for her character Lauren ('Am I bovvered?'), and also trying to break out of the mould. Another of her then outings was as the Doctor's assistant in *Doctor Who*, Donna. She, too, came in for a great deal of stick, castigated both for her choice of role and for the way she went about playing it. And although, this time round, the film was on a mainstream television channel, and so packed a few more viewers in to boost Rob's profile, that, however, was a double-edged sword.

The reviews, to put it bluntly, were awful, although some acknowledged why it could have looked like an attractive project to be involved with. 'Some people have every possible advantage in life,' wrote Matt Baylis in the *Daily Express*. 'Loving parents. A healthy body and a secure home. A good education, good looks, supportive friends. And they still turn out wrong. The same could be said of certain TV dramas. If *The Bad Mother's Handbook* had been in a packet on a supermarket shelf, I'd have stuck it in my trolley. It had so much going for it: Catherine Tate in her first serious role. It was the story of three generations of women, living uneasily together under one roof. Yet somehow, in spite of all these advantages, *The Bad Mother's Handbook* turned out to be … well, pretty bad … it was let down by two things – the surrounding characters and the dialogue.' And everything else involved, as well.

Kevin Maher in *The Times* was no more impressed, in his case pointing out that so much had been packed into the show that it was difficult to take it all seriously. 'Although *The Bad Mother's*

Handbook was not concerned with the global apocalypse, it was nonetheless heavily packed, if not burdened, with excess dramatic incident,' he wrote. 'It starred the comedian Catherine Tate (being serious, yet not quite) as an embattled supply teacher torn between an Alzheimer's-afflicted mother (Anne Reid) and a willful teenage daughter (Holly Grainger) ... The story itself seemed practically allergic to narrative downtime – in ninety minutes there was unwanted pregnancy, adoption, manslaughter, near death, birth, romance, fights and a slightly cloying resolution.' Ouch.

Did John Preston in the *Sunday Telegraph* think any better of it? He did not. '*The Bad Mother's Handbook* was a mess of a drama starring Catherine Tate as a much put-upon divorcee with a dotty mother and a stroppy teenage daughter' was how he summed it up. 'She also had an ex-husband with an atrocious false moustache. The main problem was that tonally it was all over the place. Apparently striving for emotional plausibility, it missed by several miles and eventually plumped for a familiar slurry of thin comedy, melodrama and sentimentality.'

Ally Ross, in *The Sun*, got straight down to the point. 'Rubbish,' he wrote.

The few mentions that were made of Rob weren't much better. In *The Independent*, Brian Viner describes him as playing Daniel 'as a hunchback, without the hunch'. Katie Toms in *The Observer* noted: 'Floppy-haired wally Daniel played with a little too much bumbling gusto by Robert Pattinson.' There were a couple of other similarly disobliging remarks. In truth, it wasn't his fault. The production had been panned by so many people, on so many levels, that it was clearly flawed from the start: it simply turned out that this was not the right choice for Rob to have made.

It was also the first real insight he'd had into the downside,

critically speaking, of the business he was now in, in that he had
been personally singled out for attack. It's always unpleasant to
be rubbished by the critics, but it happens in every entertainer's
career and so Rob was just going to have to learn to grow a thick
skin. Yet it also hardened him up for something else. As has
already been alluded to in the first chapter, when it was first
announced that he had been chosen for the role of Edward, fans
rose up in revolt. Taking a pasting from the critics was a dry run
for taking a pasting from the public, although in the long run,
neither was to do him any harm.

But what was he to do next? In short, it was an odd position for
such a promising young man to be in. Rob had followed up his
breakthrough role as Cedric Diggory by garnering excellent
reviews for a television film that no one watched, and lousy reviews
for something that far more people had seen and then wished they
hadn't. In the event, of course, it was to turn out all right, but
more than one up-and-coming actor has made a few iffy choices
and seen their auspicious future blow up in front of them: Rob
came closer than many people realize to being there, too. It
accounts for his lack of self-grandeur, his inability to take himself
more seriously and his self-deprecating sense of humour. He knew
it could all fade away at any moment, for at this moment, it almost
seemed that it had.

There was an upside, though. In retrospect, Rob was able to see
that this rather strange period of taking a few steps back was
ultimately to work to his advantage. 'I kind of blew it after the
Potter films,' he told the *Daily Telegraph* in 2008. 'There was a
chance for me to really kick on and use the exposure, but I didn't
really want to do anything. Looking back, it was a good thing – I
was able to teach myself how to act for a start. I could have done

some more teen movies, but I thought what was the point? I'm not all that fussed by making loads of money.'

In actual fact, of course, he was moving towards starring in the biggest teen movie of them all. As for the money – it goes with the territory. In the wake of the *Twilight* films, Rob would be in a position where he need never work again.

Not that he was quite finished with *Potter* yet, either. Rob reprised his role as Cedric Diggory in *Harry Potter and the Order of the Phoenix*, although this time only in flashbacks and recollected scenes. The story begins shortly after Cedric's death: after a summer with the Dursleys, during which Harry and his cousin Dudley are attacked by Dementors, our schoolboy hero returns to Hogwarts. As the tale grows darker still, it emerges that the Ministry of Magic and much of the wizarding world is in denial about the fact that Voldemort has returned. It has also become a crime to say that he killed Cedric. Their only hope is the Order of the Phoenix, a secret society dedicated to fighting Voldemort.

However, Cornelius Fudge, the Minister for Magic, now believes that Dumbledore is using stories about Voldemort's return to try to unseat him: he sends in a new Defence Against the Dark Arts teacher, Dolores Umbridge – who seems anything but suited to her new role – as his 'woman on the inside'. As a result, Harry and his chums set up Dumbledore's Army, so that they can learn the practical skills needed for the fight ahead. The film ends, essentially, in a battle between good and evil – and Harry gets a kiss from Cho along the way.

Although Rob's role in his second *Potter* film was much, much smaller than it had been in the previous outing, nonetheless, he was still caught up in the *Potter* machine. It was such a huge franchise that anyone who had any kind of involvement felt that their lives had been taken over, and that was certainly the case with Rob. In some ways, he felt that the sheer amount of time devoted to the *Potter* films might have held him back: all he needed to do was to go with the flow and everyone else made all his decisions for him.

'It went on for so long,' he said. 'I didn't have to decide what to do and I didn't have to do any exams or anything. It seemed like a really easy option.' And he was right. Everyone knew that the films were going to be an enormous success – after what had happened with the books, they could hardly be otherwise – and so all the actors needed to do was to show up and go along for the ride.

The experience had certainly taken it out of him, as it had all the actors involved. It is easy to forget that Rob was still relatively new to all this: still a very young man, he had only been a professional actor for four years when *Twilight* came along, and so the immensity of a shoot like *Potter* was still something new to him. It was also one of the reasons these short, arty films appealed: not only did they extend his range, but they weren't anything like as time-consuming as a blockbuster.

'My instinct at the end was just to sort of collapse,' he told *Seven* magazine of the *Potter* saga. 'What I aim to do next is a really short shoot. A six-week thing where I can get my brain round the whole thing. A play or something.' It was not the right attitude to take Hollywood by storm, but he was exhausted and needed some form of a break.

Analyse it as he later might, however, Rob gave the appearance of drifting at this juncture, unsure of where to go next. Where he actually went was back to the art house, to work on some films that were not to see the light of day until after *Twilight* was released, at which point they seemed to be even odder choices than they had been at the time. But the next year, the year in which he made those films, was to be the last period of normality Rob was to experience. For in the background, the stirrings had begun about the film of *Twilight*, and who was going to take on the lead role. Life for Rob, as he knew it back then, was never going to be the same again.

six art-house angst

As 2007 began to whizz by, Rob was still feeling relaxed, still hanging out with the up-and-coming crowd in Soho and still not entirely sure about what to do next. He'd had one television project that had garnered excellent reviews and another that had garnered rotten ones, but with the failure to capitalize on the success of *Harry Potter*, there was no longer about him that all-important 'buzz'. The *Potter* juggernaut had moved on: attention, filming-wise, had turned to the next in the series, *Harry Potter and the Half-Blood Prince*, and there was no cameo or flashback for Rob now. But the need to get cracking, to show he was still out there and capable of putting on a good performance, was becoming increasingly important. And so it was that he returned to the silver screen.

Rob was to make a trio of films before being sucked into the *Twilight* phenomenon, and given quite how different they are from the tales of the Cullens, they provide an intriguing glimpse into where Rob's career might have gone had he not landed the role of Edward. Just as he might well have ended up with a stage career, had he not lost the job at the Royal Court a couple of years earlier, so he might equally have ended up as a small-scale film actor in small-scale British films that nobody watched. Mercifully, it wasn't to be.

For these were not colossal *Potter*-esque blockbusters that Rob next signed his name to: they were art-house projects, for which Rob seemed to have discovered a taste. That predilection might have had something to do with the milieu in which he was living: Soho, with all its bohemian qualities, was more the home of films with aspirations to artistry, rather than major projects. For that level of venture, he was going to have to return to the United States.

Instead, Rob's next work was to be a film called *The Summer House*, which at the time of writing has never actually been released – although a trailer exists on YouTube – but which might achieve a release date in late 2009. Directed by Daisy Gili, the principal founder of the London Film Academy, and written by Ian Beck, who is probably best known for the novel *The Secret History of Tom Trueheart, Boy Adventurer*, the film features Rob as Richard, a self-centred young man, who is unfaithful to his girlfriend Jane, played by Talulah Riley. Jane dumps Richard and runs off to France for the summer: he follows and tries to woo her back. Bizarrely, for all Rob's avowed intentions not to find himself stereo-typed in public-school roles, Richard was very much a product of the British public-school system, with a goodly dose of unpleas-antness, conceit and unlikeability added in.

This project, like *The Bad Mother's Handbook*, probably wasn't really worthy of Rob's talents either, and, once again, his was very much a supporting role. Indeed, one of the reasons eyebrows were raised when he was eventually chosen to play Edward was that, with the exception of *The Haunted Airman* and *How to Be* (of which more later in this chapter), Rob had never played a lead before. Nor did the sulky creature he played in this film make Edward an obvious next step.

The film opens in France, where Jane is staying with her aunt, Priscilla (Anna Calder-Marshall), the widow of an author who lives off her late husband's royalties. It is the summer of 1969, which was also when the first moon landings took place, something that plays a role in the story. The movie was filmed in a beautiful location, the chateau in Douriez, near Crécy-la-Chapelle, in northern France, and this sweeping backdrop is perhaps one of the film's strongest points.

Also in situ at the lovely chateau are Freddie Porteous, played by David Burke, who was once romantically involved with Priscilla, and his chic French wife Marie Pierre, played by Marianne Borgo. This was very much a drama about the upper middle class and their agreeable interiors and lifestyles: there were certainly no working-class heroics going on here. The target audience, according to the makers of the film, was the same crowd who had enjoyed *My Summer of Love*, a tale of teenage sapphic love, which had launched the career of another British success in Hollywood, Emily Blunt.

And so, at the outset of the film, the older adults are all flirting with one another, while the younger element was nursing a broken heart. Richard turns up in the middle of this intriguing mix, determined to win back his girlfriend. The opportunity to do this comes at a party held to celebrate the moon landings: the glamorous Marie Pierre plays the Fairy Godmother to Jane's Cinderella and turns her into a sophisticated young woman, making her even more tempting to Richard.

On the night in question, Jane ventures out to the summer house of the film's title, where disillusionment sets in all round. She finds her aunt and Freddie behaving like teenagers; Richard, meanwhile, is rough and ready and, Jane realizes, not love's young dream after all. She burns the unopened letters he has sent her and drops them into a well.

Sulky and smouldering, Rob bears a curious resemblance to the young Mick Jagger in the film. Indeed, his character, a nasty piece of work, really is entirely self-regarding: he has only taken up with Jane in the first place because he wants a trophy girlfriend, and only wants her back again because he can't take being dumped. When he doesn't immediately get what he wants, he turns on her: in all, he is a most unappealing character – and another slightly odd role for Rob to choose. This was a small-scale art-house film, hardly the natural follow-up after all the *Potter* fuss, nor a set-the-world-alight choice in the wake of the *Bad Mother's Handbook* debacle. But at least it gave him an agreeable break in France.

Ironically, *The Summer House* was to become yet another project that is remembered primarily because it features Rob. On the imdb.com website, the premier source of film information on the web, the cast list features only one picture of the actors involved – and it's of Rob. On the numerous Rob fan sites on the web, there are several threads discussing how to get hold of the film. As with all Rob's ventures at this time, what appeared in the moment to be minute projects, compared to what could have been on offer in Hollywood, in retrospect had a huge light cast on them because of the involvement of one of their minor players. In each case, the casting directors' decision had been cleverer than they had known.

But it was not high-profile work, and nor was the next film on the cards. Sporting another atrocious haircut – all lank, misshapen locks falling about his face – Rob now took part in another indie movie, *How to Be*, written and directed by Oliver Irving, and co-starring Mike Pearce and Johnny White. In the film, Rob plays the leading role of Art, a twenty-something musician who is dumped by his girlfriend: he moves back in with his parents and then his problems really begin. To give some indication of the mood of the piece, the film opens with Art remembering how his father burnt all his 'magical' toys in the family back garden when he was a child. And then the tone gets more downbeat still.

Art is a musician (like Rob) who plays the guitar, but try as he might, he can't actually complete any work of music. He is asked to leave his job as a volunteer in a community centre. He tries to start up a rock band with a friend, Ronny, but since the friend is agoraphobic and can't venture out, that comes to nothing, too.

Not a single aspect of his life goes to plan. Art's relationship with his parents is hideous: that won't come right, no matter what he does to improve it. He begs his girlfriend to return to him: she doesn't. This is a full-on 'quarter-life crisis'. Art sums it up by saying, 'I just feel unhappy all the time.' (So, by this time, does the viewer.)

Matters finally take a turn for the better when he reads *It's Not Your Fault*, a book by the self-help guru Dr Levi Ellington (Powell Jones), and hires the author to make him, Art, more normal, bringing Levi over from Canada in the process.

All in all, it was yet another departure from the norm. It premiered at the twelfth Rhode Island International Film Festival, to a slightly muted reaction: while there was general agreement that the film had been very well made, it wasn't half gloomy. And there was a real problem in that the viewer sometimes wanted to shake Art and tell him to get a grip. There wasn't a great deal any actor could have done under the circumstances, but no one could claim that this was Rob's finest hour.

'The sight of Ellington turning up in the most unlikely places – a children's restroom at a school, for instance – adds a light touch to the film,' said the *Providence Journal*. 'Yet even though Pattinson is very good at playing a man who is all at sea in his life, the character of Arthur is so hopelessly frustrating and pathetic that his inability to move forward may be equally frustrating for the audience.'

Although it will never be seen as one of his major works, this film may well have been what persuaded Rob to choose acting as the path he really wanted to take. He played the guitar in the film, and sang, showing himself to be an increasingly accomplished musician, of which much more anon. But while music was to remain a crucial part of his life, in the end it couldn't compete with acting.

The director, Oliver Irving, certainly thought Rob was perfect for the role – and not just because of his musical skills. As with the casting of Edward, Rob's unique qualities, that seem to burn on-screen, singled him out instantly for the job. 'We did auditions for this for well over a year in bursts,' Irving told the website Pattinson Music. 'I feel like I must have seen every young male actor in London! I was looking for someone who would work well with the other actors I had in place to play Art's friends. These were non-actors whose approach had been tailored while we made home movies over the years, so the actor for Art needed not to seem like he had been to drama school. Rob has said that at the time he was thinking of giving up acting and pursuing music as he was unhappy with roles he was getting offered – but pretty much straight away I knew he was right for the part. He had a sort of playful energy, perhaps even naivety, which he brought to the part and he really seemed to understand the characters.'

This was also the first time Rob had performed as a musician as well as an actor. It is well known that music is a great interest of his, and something he has considered pursuing professionally. *How to Be* marked his musical debut on film, and in some very memorable scenes. 'There is a great "jam session" sequence where Ronny is playing his electronic stuff and Art is strumming away soulfully on the guitar, while Nikki is singing away about random things,' Oliver continued. 'It was very funny to shoot and painful to watch!'

Joe Hastings, the composer on the film, agreed with Irving's endorsement. 'Rob brought a kind of ownership to the music,' he said. 'Before the part was cast, I was unsure as to whether someone could make the tracks seem real. I think Rob genuinely enjoyed playing the songs.'

Hastings also elaborated on the instruments Rob played in the film: 'Rob played a battered old nylon string acoustic which Oliver "acquired" from a school; we found a piece of rope in the studios we used as a set and decided that it would make the perfect guitar strap for Art. For the final sequence, we deliberately chose a flashy if slightly tacky guitar made by Ovation. It was one of those bowl-backed fibreglass types that I hate, they're the nouveau riche's guitar of choice.' But it worked in the film.

The character of Art is actually something of a lost soul: partly torn apart by anger and partly unable to move through fear; in all, thoroughly disillusioned with the world. Rob gave depth to his portrayal of the character and the film garnered very mixed reviews when it finally came out in 2009 – not on general release, but via an on-demand process.

'Beginning with the most insipidly unusual and unforgivingly cold of familial circumstances, Art's hopeless effort at making his place in the small world of those around him is devastating' is what the *Examiner* had to say about it. 'Nearly deserving tears from your eyes, Art suffers an alienation and endlessness in struggle that leaves one bitter and completely sympathetic.'

Nor were the critics going to shy away from who was really going to go and see the film, drawing very similar conclusions from the release of this film and a few more made before Rob hit the big time. 'Originally just a twee British indie that won a minor prize at the 2008 Slamdance Film Festival, *How to Be* suddenly became something more when Pattinson turned into an overnight sensation last year with his role in blockbuster vampire romance *Twilight,*' said Geoff Berkshire in *Metromix*. 'Fortunately for everyone involved, viewership will likely be limited to Pattinson's hard-core fans, happy to see a movie simply because he's in it. His performance is adequate – nothing special but nothing embarrassing – and it won't hurt that the role perfectly fits the introverted, awkward artist persona he's cultivated in the media. Fans who love "RPattz" even more than Edward Cullen should be satisfied. They'll be the only ones.'

It could be said that this was an atypical review, but in fact, the film got hardly any reviews at all. One of the few others, from Steve Rhodes on *Internet Reviews*, is similarly acidic: 'Filled with British humour so dry it's downright parched,' he wrote. 'Still, if you're a big fan of Robert Pattinson, I suspect you won't be disappointed.'

It wasn't Rob's finest hour, but once again he had acquitted himself well when faced with a new challenge. And though the reviews were hardly glowing, most commented broadly on the film itself. The comments on Rob personally, while muted, seemed to concur that he had delivered an acceptable performance, one that fans would appreciate and that could not be unfairly dismissed as rubbish. In the wake of *Twilight*'s overwhelming success, the

The young
Robert Pattinson.

Playing with his sister – that day, at least,
the slide was more interesting than 'Claudia'.

Taking a stroll with his mum, Clare.

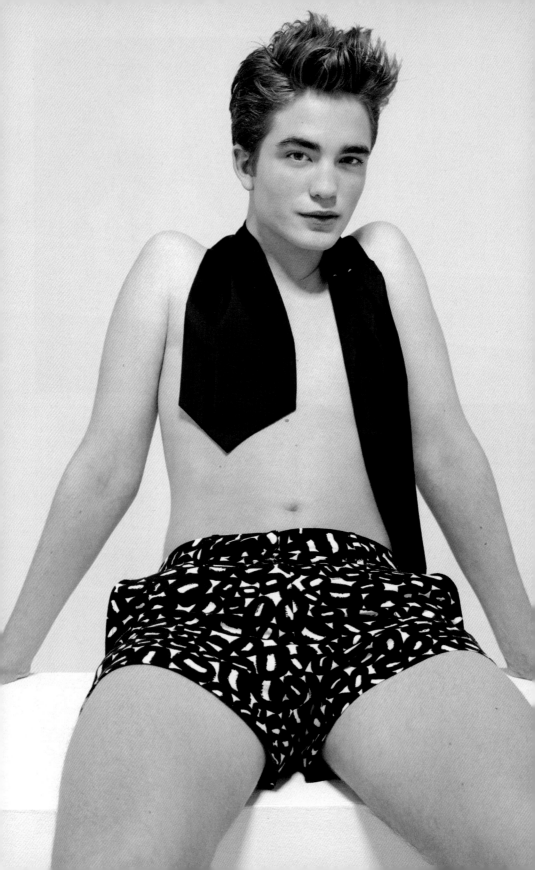

(Vi)king of the world:
as Giselher in *Ring of the Nibelungs*.

Facing page: Rob the model.

From one schoolboy
to another: Rob's
school picture from
Tower House (above),
and as Cedric
Diggory in *Harry
Potter and the Goblet
of Fire* (left).

Cedric was Rob's first major film role. Here he is at work on set with director Mike Newell.

At a photo call with the stars of *Goblet*.
From left to right: (back row) Katie Leung,
Stanislav Ianevski, Clemence Poesy, Rob;
Rupert Grint, Daniel Radcliffe, Emma Watson.

Red devil: Rob walks
the red carpet at the
Potter premiere – with
standout star quality.

Bad hair day or *The Bad Mother's Handbook*?

Rob in indie flick *How to Be*.
In a demonstration of his musical talents,
Rob sang three songs in this film.

Portrait of the artist: as Salvador Dali in
Little Ashes.

Hold on to your hats: the *Twilight* roller coaster begins at Comic-Con 2008. The cast from left to right: Edi Gathegi, Cam Gigandet, Rob, Kristen Stewart, Taylor Lautner, Rachelle Lefevre.

Rising star: Rob at the 2008 Hollywood Film Festival with actress Camilla Belle, clutching his prestigious New Hollywood Award.

Opposite page and overleaf: Rob and Kristen launch *Twilight* at the Rome International Film Festival.

spotlight on Rob was burning fiercely bright. It was little wonder critics were judging his early work with hawk-eyed precision – but all the more reassuring that, despite that increased attention, Rob's work was proving very difficult to slate.

There was one last outing, made in the pre-*Twilight* days, and released after it, that was to demonstrate once and for all that Rob was a man determined to make his mark as an actor, who was adamant he would not simply be known for his (very pretty) face. This was a film called *Little Ashes*. If Rob was out to prove he was more than just a teen heart-throb – and really, that had been apparent through all his kooky career choices – then he couldn't have done better than to choose this. He was to play the artist Salvador Dali, complete with silly moustache; even more controversially, this version of Salvador Dali was to be gay.

Dali was one of the great eccentrics of the twentieth century. A Spanish surrealist artist, Dali painted many of the famous 'dream' paintings, in which, for example, solid objects seemed to melt. In later years, however, he became more famous for his very mannered appearance – especially that luxuriant moustache – than anything else.

Little Ashes was actually the title of a painting by Dali: the film was to be directed by Paul Morrison, written by Philippa Goslett, and set in 1920s Madrid. (It is notable that the vast majority of Rob's films up to this point are not set in the present day.) It centred on a trio of men: Dali, the surrealist film-maker Luis Buñuel (played by Matthew McNulty), and the Spanish playwright and poet Federico García Lorca (played by Javier Beltrán).

In the course of the movie, Dali and Lorca attempt, ultimately unsuccessfully, to have an affair, although critics were quick to point out that in real life, nothing of the sort ever took place. It was another art-house offering on a miniscule budget of £1.4 million (which would probably not even have covered the *Harry Potter* cast and crew catering costs).

There was a background to this imagined relationship, however. In 1969 (the year in which *The Summer House* was set), a pamphlet was published called *Alain Bosquet's Conversations with Dali*. Bosquet was a French surrealist poet who had known Dali, and it was his memories of the Dali–Lorca dynamic that formed the basis of the new film, for they addressed this exact issue. Relaying a conversation he had had with the painter, Bosquet transcribed Dali's comments about Lorca: '"He was homosexual, as everyone knows, and madly in love with me," Dali said. "He tried to screw me twice … I was extremely annoyed, because I wasn't homosexual, and I wasn't interested in giving in. So nothing came of it. But I felt awfully flattered vis-à-vis the prestige. Deep down, I felt that he was a great poet."'

The writer of the script, Philippa Goslett, felt that, on the strength of these admissions, at the very least an emotional attachment had clearly taken place between Dali and Lorca. 'Having done a huge amount of research, it's clear something happened, no question,' she said to *The Guardian*. 'When you look at the letters, it's clear something more was going on there. It began as a friendship, became more intimate and moved to a physical level, but Dali found it difficult and couldn't carry on. Considering Dali's massive hang-ups, it's not surprising.'

In truth, it is slightly immaterial as to whether there was any veracity behind the making of the film: it should really be judged as a work on its own merits. The trouble was that when the critics came to do so, they weren't much impressed by what they saw.

At the beginning of the film, Dali is eighteen, newly arrived in

Madrid in 1922. He takes up residence in the Residencia de Estudiantes, a university halls, where he meets Buñuel and Lorca. He later described Lorca as 'the poetic phenomenon incarnate', and the only person who ever made him jealous (of his talent, not for any other reason). Lorca was unquestionably gay, but in this version of events, the two men develop a friendship, which deepens into a love affair. However, Dali finds it impossible to consummate this romance and so, as some form of compensation, Lorca sleeps with a woman, while Dali watches. *Harry Potter* it wasn't.

Goslett tried to explain the resonance of that love-making scene between Lorca and a woman. 'Lorca slept with a female friend of theirs, which Dali called the ultimate sacrifice,' she said. 'Dali watched it and this was the start of his voyeurism. It was the construction of his mask that we are familiar with now. For me, the real tragedy is Dali. He was really haunted by Lorca for the rest of his life and talked about him incessantly – more than his wife, Gala.'

To say that this was a departure for Rob doesn't even begin to describe it, but it was a far cannier choice than it seemed at first. By this time, he knew he was in the running for the role of another schoolboy, one that was pretty different from Cedric Diggory, admittedly, but another teen heart-throb nonetheless. And so he knew it was crucial that he showed he could do more than look handsome with cheekbones – hence this very challenging, strange role.

'I didn't want to get stuck in pretty, public-school roles, or I knew I'd end up as some sort of caricature,' he told *ES* magazine. 'Playing Dali has been a complete turning point for me. It's the first part I've had that has required really serious thought. I became completely obsessed with Dali during the filming, and I read every biography I could get hold of. He was the most bizarre, complex man, but in the end I felt I could relate to him.'

Reading between the lines, however, it's not impossible to surmise that Rob came to regret making this film, or at the very least had decided that it was the big productions he now wanted to work in, not something that most people would never bother to see. At the time he made *Little Ashes*, Rob was learning his trade, and how to dig deep into the character he was acting. Like everyone else, of course, at that moment he had no idea exactly what was going to happen next; that he would be catapulted from near obscurity into a globally famous star. And so this peculiar little art-house offering, released as it was after *Twilight* came out, seemed a very odd choice of vehicle for someone who was now as famous as Rob.

He, harking back to the tactlessness he'd shown when first talking about the role of Cedric, appeared to think so too, unwisely at one point dismissing the film as 'nothing' and adding, 'We didn't even have trailers.' This did not go down well with the film's bosses, who insisted Rob go out there and explain himself.

This incident was brought up in an interview with *The Guardian* in spring 2009, when the film was eventually released in the UK. Rob exploded briefly, something else his film bosses presumably didn't much like either. 'I hate having to do all this shit!' he told the startled interviewer. 'I've already been told to apologize for saying it. I was just trying to say that it was a tiny, little film. It had a miniscule budget. I was just trying to say that if *Twilight* hadn't come along, I don't know how much *Little Ashes* would have been publicized. In an ideal world, everyone would go around watching art-house films about Dali and Lorca. But a lot of people have no idea who Lorca even was.'

It was hard to escape the conclusion that the pressure was getting to him – and by this stage, the pressure on Rob was huge. There was also the added element that having just turned into a teen idol, he was of course in this film playing someone who was gay, or who was, at least, tempted by the idea of a gay affair. Rob had to tread very carefully there, too. What he could not express, for fear of incurring the wrath of the gay-rights lobby, was any indication that he might have been concerned about his young female fans seeing him in a gay sex scene (although, as it turned out, it didn't seem to put any of them off). Rob was all too aware that any slightly downbeat or disparaging comment could – and probably would – be taken the wrong way: 'People love all the negative stuff – "He doesn't like the film!" "He's a homophobe!" Oh great.'

Although clearly neither was the case, Rob kept making matters worse. At the time of the interview, he confessed that he had only recently seen *Little Ashes* for the first time – but admittedly, he never liked watching himself on-screen. 'It's like self-flagellation, so why should I bother?' he explained. 'And I didn't want to piss on anyone's grave. It was hard to watch my first scene, in which I turn up in this funny little hat.' He did go some way towards redeeming himself on all fronts, however, with his next comment: 'I was worried about watching them, but Dali and Lorca's sex scenes were in fact the best scenes.'

His thoughts on the small-scale movie revealed a marked change in attitude to some years previously, and an indication that Rob was now becoming fully immersed in the world of the blockbuster, the Hollywood epic and all the magic of the truly vast productions on the silver screen. Just four years previously, in the wake of the *Harry Potter* filming, he had appeared to have a very different take on it all. Productions don't come much bigger than *Potter*, and Rob had sounded almost exhausted by it all. He liked the films of the 1970s, he told *Seven* magazine, 'When you could just make a film for nothing. There's no reason why a film should cost $100 million. It's crazy. People will say, "We'll fly you out there to some country, pay all your living expenses, and then we'll pay you." You're just like, why? I'm not really sure what my point is ... I don't want to be paid ever again? I hate money? I want to do anything for free!'

'No, he doesn't,' said his publicist, who was present. It was a lesson Rob had clearly learned by 2009.

Little Ashes was eventually released in May 2009, six months after the premiere of *Twilight*. The general consensus was that Rob was better off playing vampires.

'Paul Morrison's film about the student-days friendship of Dali, Lorca and Buñuel falls into the trap that claims nearly all biopics of bohemian artists: everybody speaks in potted manifestos, delivered with much flouncy waving of cigarettes,' wrote Edward Porter in *The Times*. 'Morrison adopts the silly compromise of having the characters speak English dialogue with a Spanish accent. That aside, they might as well be wandering around Oxford with Sebastian Flyte ... The only viewers on whom the film is likely to make a big impression are young fans of Robert Pattinson, the heart-throb star of *Twilight*. For them, watching their idol's unrestrained performance as Dali will be quite a crash course in surrealism.'

Xan Brooks, in *The Guardian*, agreed. 'Dali is played (a trifle uncertainly) by *Twilight* star Robert Pattinson, although Paul Morrison's film was actually shot before it,' he observed. 'Its belated release is presumably based on the not-unreasonable assumption that a significant number of teenaged fans will be prepared to endure a low-budget period romance on the understanding that they will, at some stage, get to see their idol in the buff.'

Even there, though, they risked disappointment. When Rob got the role of Edward, he worked out intensively with a personal trainer for some months before filming began. In *Little Ashes*, he cuts an altogether more slender figure.

Nor was Tim Robey, in the *Daily Telegraph*, very impressed. 'Trying out, then taking off, a series of loony ensembles and hairstyles, *Twilight* pin-up Robert Pattinson goes for broke as the young Salvador Dali – he's terribly intense and Christopher Walken-ish – in this weirdly sketchy and underpopulated biographical drama, which pivots around the artist's supposed gay semi-affair with Lorca (the much more charismatic Javier Beltrán),' he opined. 'Meanwhile, their pal Buñuel (Matthew McNulty) – homophobe first, legendary director second, here – scowls from the sidelines. Director Paul Morrison (*Wondrous Oblivion*) doesn't do a terrible job on the budget, but it's all a good deal too amateur-*Brideshead* to be believed.'

Some reviewers were a little more kind, observing that it took some guts for Rob to take on the role. But they, too, predicted that it was the fans of the very different movie he made shortly afterwards who would actually be filling the cinemas. 'A look at the early life of painter Salvador Dali, *Little Ashes* is an art-house film filled with bare bottoms, full-frontal nudity and gay passion. You can practically hear Pattinson's army of girl fans weeping into their popcorn,' wrote David Edwards in the *Daily Mirror*. 'Full credit to Pattinson for trying something so completely different – and he does a decent job, even if you're never able to quite buy into it.'

Matthew Turner on viewlondon.co.uk was also more generous. 'The film is beautifully shot throughout, courtesy of Adam Suschitzky's lush cinematography and some impeccable production design work' was his view. 'Similarly, the performances are excellent and there's strong chemistry between Pattinson and Beltrán – their first kiss is surprisingly romantic.'

One of the problems was that, yet again, Rob was let down by his hair, which was slicked back and played down in an attempt to tone down its buoyant nature. In fact, it can be loosely observed that Rob's hairstyle tended to mirror the success of the film he was in: when it was lush and abundant, the film was likewise (*Harry Potter*; *Twilight*), and when it was a complete mess, so too was the vehicle it appeared in (*The Bad Mother's Handbook*).

And in this case, his appearance was made worse by his moustache. Salvador Dali had one of the most famous moustaches of the twentieth century, and so Rob sported an approximation of the original. It certainly didn't do anything for him – quite the opposite, in fact. As Kurt Loder at MTV unkindly but accurately pointed out, 'As soon as Pattinson steps forth with Dali's famous up-twirled moustache pasted to his face, the picture collapses.' That was, alas, very much the case.

In all, Rob's ventures into small and independent productions had been disappointing. Although the freedom of projects such as *How to Be* had made him both appreciate acting and its capacity to facilitate and complement his other passion – music – with the possible exception of *The Haunted Airman*, he had not found a vehicle to do him justice.

In retrospect, it can be said that it was as well that he got this period out of his system when he did, however. After all, he had relatively little to lose: in the wake of playing Edward, had he made the same career choices, it would have produced absolute bafflement in the industry. As it was, when these small-scale films came out in the aftermath of his fame, there was some degree of understanding that he'd been a good sport to have a go.

Of course, Rob didn't spend this entire time working. There was some play, too. But crucially, according to Rob himself, there was no girlfriend on the scene. For an actor who has inspired such devotion, Rob has spent surprisingly long amounts of time being single. In fact, he was later to claim that, during this period, whenever he asked a girl out, she just didn't want to know. (His complaint was going to be exactly the opposite post-celebrity, as then he was to say that it would be impossible to date anyone, given the scrutiny he was under – although that certainly didn't stop the gossips from constantly pairing him off.) Judging from his own words, he just wasn't getting the girls at this point. Fast-forward a few months, and the ones that managed to get anywhere near him were practically shredding him apart.

Rob's life was on the verge of a massive change. He was single, with no particular reason to stay in London if he didn't want to, and fairly sure by now that it was acting he wanted to pursue, not music. Where would he turn next? He had, of course, got all the accoutrements of a professional actor at this stage, including agents on both sides of the Atlantic: Sarah Spear and Grace Clissold at the prestigious Curtis Brown agency in the UK, and Stephanie Ritz, of the Endeavor Agency, in the United States.

In autumn 2007, when Rob was dabbling in his art-house movies, uncertain of his career path, and concentrating more on hanging out in Soho than anything else, his American agent got a whiff of a new role that would be coming up in the following year. It was as the lead character in the first *Twilight* movie, and it was already apparent that whoever got this role was to become a massive star.

The producers had not yet made any choices about who the lucky actor was going to be, and Stephanie Ritz had an idea that she had someone on her books who might just fit the bill. There were various problems related to this brainwave, namely that he was not American and, with *Potter* now lost in the mists of time, and only some very small-scale work done since then, no one had ever heard of him.

No one was more dubious than Rob himself when Stephanie put the idea to him, but she had utter faith in her client. Could it be true? Could Rob really be about to land the role of his life?

seven
twilight falls

The publishing industry had never seen anything like it – well, since the success of the *Harry Potter* series, at least. The year was 2008, and a set of books about a vampire who had fallen in love with a human girl had sold over 22 million copies – in that year alone. The first novel of the quartet, *Twilight*, had been the bestselling book of the past twelve months. Indeed, by mid 2009, the *Twilight* series, which features the couple and their forbidden romance, had sold over 42 million copies worldwide, with translations into thirty-seven languages, one film of the first book already in the bag and the next on its way.

That the *Twilight* series was a phenomenon, there was no doubt. Stephenie Meyer, the author of the books, related that their inspiration came to her in a dream – on 2 June 2003, to be precise: she had fallen asleep and dreamed of a vampire, who both loved a young human girl but at the same time thirsted for her blood. So vivid was the dream that despite having never published a book before, Stephenie first turned her imaginings into words (this is now chapter thirteen of the first novel, with Bella and Edward in the meadow), and then wrote a whole account of what she had imagined.

'I already knew he was a vampire and he was sparkly and beautiful and she was just kind of ordinary and in awe of this creature,' Stephenie told *The Times*. 'He was explaining how hard it was not to kill her and she was amazed that he wanted to be around her even if it was risking her life.'

Stephenie couldn't stop thinking about this strange dream, and began writing it up that very day. 'Where would it go next?' she continued. 'Would he kill her or would they work it out? I just thought about it until I had to make breakfast. The dream is what started me off. I had fun that day. It was just ten pages. I didn't think about writing it as a book, I just wanted to see what happened next. I know when I started writing because I had it marked on my calendar. That was the day I started my summer diet and it was the first day of swimming lessons for the kids.'

She had a complete manuscript after just three months. Matters moved fast: Stephenie signed a three-book deal with Little, Brown and Company for $750,000 and the book was published in 2005, the same year that Rob made his debut in the *Harry Potter* films.

Stephenie – a little like J. K. Rowling, who certainly didn't stand out from the crowd until she became a mega-selling author – went from being just another ordinary person on the street to a literary superstar practically overnight. Born on 24 December 1973 in Hartford, Connecticut, to Stephen and Candy Morgan, Stephenie was brought up in Phoenix, Arizona, as a member of The Church of Jesus Christ of Latter-day Saints, more commonly known as Mormons.

Her father Stephen worked as the chief financial officer of a contracting firm; it was a standard, middle-class upbringing. She had five brothers and sisters, Seth, Emily, Jacob, Paul and Heidi (*Twilight* aficionados will recognize the names of several characters in the books in that list), and went on to study English at the Brigham Young University in Provo, Utah.

Stephenie met Christian Meyer, who is always known as Pancho, when she was still very young, and she married young, too, in 1995, at the age of twenty-one. Before giving birth to the literary series that has since beguiled the world, she had her flesh-and-blood family: Gabe, Seth and Eli. She was simply a perfectly ordinary Mormon housewife, until the *Twilight* saga changed her life.

Stephenie remains a practising Mormon: she doesn't drink alcohol or watch adult films, and her beliefs actually play a significant part in understanding the books. 'We have free will, which is a huge gift from God,' she told the *New York Times* in an interview in April 2008. 'If you tie that up with something like, I don't know, cocaine, then you don't really have a lot of freedom anymore.' This applies directly to Edward and the rest of the Cullens: although they desire human blood, they have made the moral choice not to drink it, and sate themselves with animals, instead.

Of course, this applies to Edward more than any of them. Although he sees himself as a monster, the reader knows he is actually good, as we watch him struggling constantly with what he wants to do as opposed to what he knows he should do. 'I really think that's the underlying metaphor of my vampires,' Stephenie continued. 'It doesn't matter where you're stuck in life or what you think you have to do; you can always choose something else. There's always a different path.'

The characters in the *Twilight* series are not, of course, Mormons, but they live by other Mormon precepts, as well. Many teenagers drink and smoke: not this crowd. There's also no sex, partly because Edward is afraid that he would get carried away and accidentally kill Bella rather than make love to her (and in that dark impulse lies the making of all the great romantic heroes:

to be so overcome with passion that they can't control themselves), and partly because thwarted desire is always more sexy than sated lust.

And on top of that, the author herself wouldn't approve. 'I got some pressure to put a big sex scene in,' Stephenie told the *New York Times*. 'But you can go anywhere for graphic sex. It's harder to find a romance where they dwell on the hand-holding. I was a late bloomer. When I was sixteen, holding hands was just – wow.'

Then, of course, there's Bella, the other central character in the novels. Bella is an unusual protagonist, in that she doesn't exactly stand out from the crowd: everything about her is ordinary, just as everything about the Cullens is extraordinary. This, according to the author herself, is another key to the books' success.

'I didn't realize the books would appeal to people so broadly,' Stephenie told *Entertainment Weekly*. 'I think some of it's because Bella is an "everygirl". She's not a hero, and she doesn't know the difference between Prada and whatever else is out there. She doesn't always have to be cool, or wear the coolest clothes ever. She's normal. And there aren't a lot of girls in literature that are normal. Another thing is that Bella's a good girl, which is just sort of how I imagine teenagers, because that's how my teenage years were.' That Mormon upbringing was never far away.

Of course, another of the ways in which Stephenie's beliefs inform her writing is when it comes down to the notion of the soul. As Bella slowly begins to realize that the only way she and Edward can stay together in perpetuity – and indeed, stay at the same age – is if she, too, becomes a vampire, at the same time Edward won't countenance it, because he believes he would be destroying her soul. Whether or not this would actually be the case is never made clear, but the point is that it is what Edward believes, and is another moral choice he must make. He wants Bella for eternity, and could have her for just that, but if he gives in to that desire, then he destroys something, so he believes, within her. Not for nothing is this the ultimate case of forbidden love.

All these religious implications found their way onto the cover of *Twilight*, which is illustrated with a picture of an apple – forbidden fruit (for the apple is the fruit associated with the temptation Eve offered Adam in the Garden of Eden). For books that are allegedly for teenagers, these are remarkably adult themes; not to mention, of course, their *Potter*-esque obsession with burgeoning teen sexuality. The fact that we perhaps read rather too much about Ron's teen fumblings in the *Potter* series and not very much at all about Edward's in *Twilight* is proof that in many cases less really is more.

Stephenie herself professes surprise that people talk so much about her religion. In fact, the Mormon faith is still a minority one, not practised by many people, and of those who do, the vast majority live in the United States, and so it is not actually too amazing that it's a talking point – the most famous Mormon prior to Stephenie was probably Donny Osmond. But Stephenie continues to find it strange.

'It seems funny that it's still a story, because you didn't hear people saying, "Jon Stewart, Jewish writer," when his book came out,' she told *USA Today*. 'I guess being a Mormon is just odd enough that people think it's still a real story. Obviously, to me, it seems supernormal. It's just my religion.'

The books, and more recently the films, have all borne a strong comparison with the *Harry Potter* series, involving as they do teenagers battling evil, the supernatural, and a strange world hidden right under the noses of ordinary mortals, to say nothing of the fact that the same actor, Rob, appears in both series. But there are all sorts of parallels as well, including what happened to their creators: both authors turned into superstars.

Like J. K. Rowling before her, as the success of the books grew, Stephenie started to get mobbed at public appearances. Tickets for her readings sold out overnight. It seemed almost symbolic when *Eclipse*, the third novel in the series, was published in 2007: it knocked *Harry Potter and the Deathly Hallows* off the number-one spot. It was as if the baton was being handed from one woman to the next. Stephenie, understandably, was cautious about the comparison: 'There will never be another J. K. Rowling,' she told *USA Today*. 'I'm just happy being Stephenie Meyer. That's cool enough for me.' And indeed, her sales have still not quite matched the woman who went before her – but she has only five books out, compared to the seven that make up the *Harry Potter* series. The race is not run yet.

Twilight, the novel that set it all off, was first published in 2005: what follows contains spoilers for the plot of this book and the subsequent ones. It introduces Isabella 'Bella' Swan: like Stephenie, she lives in Phoenix, Arizona, a town awash with sunshine. However, when her mother, Renée, remarries – Bella's parents are divorced – out of a sense of duty, Bella returns to live with her father, Charlie, in Forks, Washington, a town she has never liked because of the lack of sunlight and the constant presence of rain. (Stephenie had never actually been to the town herself when she wrote the book, but Googled US annual rainfall to find her setting.)

Bella enrolls in the local high school, and on the first day finds herself sitting next to the stratospherically handsome Edward Cullen, part of the Cullen family. These five teenagers have been adopted by a doctor at the local hospital and his wife, both of whom are also almost unfeasibly attractive. The Cullen siblings stand out from everyone else at the school, partly because they are so astonishingly good-looking, but also because they are so aloof. Edward, however, is more than aloof to Bella: his behaviour is that of a man who loathes her, and she catches him asking to change classes so he will not have to sit beside her. The other boys react quite differently to her, with Bella, for the first time in her life, becoming the object of constant male attention. Only Edward seems immune, although he does begin to loosen up.

Their relationship changes completely one day when Bella is in the school car park. One of her fellow students' vans careers towards her, out of control, and although Bella had quite clearly seen Edward on the other side of the car park, almost immediately and inexplicably, he is beside her, pulling her out of harm's way. Even more puzzlingly, he actually manages to stop the van, using sheer force. Bella realizes that Edward, like the rest of the Cullens, is clearly not all he seems.

She begins to get to the heart of the mystery after she visits the Native American reservation outside of town and talks to Jacob Black, an old family friend and one of the other major characters in the story. He tells her local tribal legends about a band of people who are ancient enemies with his own tribe; he hints that the Cullens are these people, and that his forebears made a pact with them never to trespass on each other's land. The Native Americans themselves have ancient secrets, but by now Bella has worked out the truth – that the Cullens are actually vampires.

As Bella's relationship with Edward develops, she discovers she is right. More than that, she also learns that his initial behaviour to her, so seemingly hostile, was enacted because he had desperately wanted to drink her blood – more than with any other human he had ever previously encountered – but then, paradoxically, had fallen passionately in love with her. Afraid that his baser instincts would overcome him, he feared he would harm her, and so attempted to keep a distance between them. In the end, of course, he was unable to stay away from her. The two become increasingly intertwined, although the physical contact between them is minimal, for whenever they try to embrace, Edward's bloodlust starts to get out of hand.

Bella discovers that vampires do not eat or sleep, and have cold, granite-like skin. She also learns why they have chosen to live in rainy, grey Forks: when a vampire is exposed to the sun, he or she does not disintegrate, as in the legend, but sparkles – so brightly it is impossible to remain hidden from prying, human eyes. The Cullens avoid human blood, going hunting for animals instead, whom they pursue on foot as they can run at great speed. Edward's 'superpower' is also revealed: he can read minds – but, puzzlingly, he cannot read Bella's.

Introduced to the rest of the Cullens, who are aware she knows their secret, Bella accompanies the family to a baseball game deep in the heart of the forest, where disaster strikes. Another coven of vampires becomes aware of them and, having approached to ask if they can join in the game, realizes there is a human in their midst. 'You brought a snack?' one of the vampires, Laurent, asks.

The Cullens are able to protect Bella initially, but it soon becomes apparent that another of the vampires, James, is determined to hunt her down. The Cullens split into two groups in an attempt to distract him: the gentle Alice Cullen, who can see into the future (not always accurately, which goes on to cause problems in itself), and Jasper take Bella to Phoenix, to hide. There she receives a phone call from James, telling her he has her mother captive. Although she knows it will result in her death, Bella goes to meet him, to save her mother's life.

When Bella arrives at the ballet school where they have arranged to rendezvous, she discovers she has been tricked: James does not have Renée at all and her quest will result only in her own death. James attacks her, but at the very last moment the Cullens arrive, pull him off her and kill him. It is only then that anyone realizes that James has bitten Bella: Edward sucks the vampire venom from her hand before she can become like him.

After a stay in hospital, Bella returns to Forks, where she begins to appreciate some uncomfortable truths. It finally sinks in that Edward, although he is aged 108, looks seventeen and always will. Unlike Bella herself, he will never grow old: so they have only a very limited time during which they are physically the same age. She also realizes that the only way they can stay together forever is if she, too, becomes a vampire. At the high-school prom, she asks Edward to bite her. He will not.

The character of Edward was going to offer an actor the role of a lifetime; that much was clear. What would be particularly challenging was not so much the physical stunts that the man who played Edward would have to perform – as special effects can make almost anything possible these days – but the heightened sense of emotion throughout this and the later books. Edward carries a strong sense of self-loathing, which would require a very finely nuanced performance indeed, for Edward has nothing to loathe himself for. Inside the books, within the terms of the story, Edward believes he doesn't have a soul; outside them, to the readers, he appears an enormously attractive character. It would be a huge task to pull that off.

Then there is the constant sense of unfulfilled longing throughout: again a massive challenge to bring to the screen. Edward was not the sort of character who could be brought to life by a conventional 'action man' actor – the young Arnold Schwarzenegger, for example, would probably not have done justice to the role – but only by someone who was capable of bringing a sense of yearning for something unattainable to the part, and then communicating that via film, often with very little dialogue at his disposal. This also applied to Bella, which is why, when it came to casting the film, the chemistry between the two central actors was considered to be more important than anything else.

Appearance, which Rob was to hark back to over and over again once he got the role, played a part, too. Edward was not only tortured and brooding, he was physically perfect, which set up yet another dilemma as far as the film-makers were concerned. Many very good-looking young actors are only too aware that they're very good-looking – and, as such, have a certain swagger about their demeanour, which would have been utterly wrong for Edward. Rob, on the other hand, despite the male modelling days, has to this day never given the impression that he does anything other than sigh when he looks in the mirror. His modesty would turn out to be crucial to his interpretation.

When *Twilight*, the book, came out, though, all that was a long way off. From the start, however, it caused a sensation, much like *Harry Potter*, turning its author from complete unknown into major celebrity overnight. Of course, there has always been something sexy about vampires, given that their chosen method of dispatching their victims is by biting their necks, but there was an even greater quality to this one, a good vampire who will fight with himself in order to save the woman he loves from harm.

And then there was the element of all-consuming love. Much has been made of Bella's total obsession with Edward, not least by female writers tut-tutting about women who love their men too much, but it's absolutely clear that Edward is equally obsessed with Bella in return. And the forbidden element to it all only added to the appeal: how could this particular couple ever be together?

The book got excellent reviews on the whole. *The Times* said it captured 'perfectly the teenage feeling of sexual tension and alienation'. According to Amazon.com, it was 'deeply romantic and extraordinarily suspenseful'. *Publishers Weekly* highlighted the way the romance flawlessly illustrated the sexual frustration that accompanies adolescence; and even the reviews that were less than wholly positive admitted the book contained elements that made for a compulsive read.

'There are some flaws here – a plot that could have been tightened, an over-reliance on adjectives and adverbs to bolster dialogue – but this dark romance seeps into the soul,' said *Booklist*. The most negative review came from *Kirkus*, and even it acknowledged this was not just another teen romance: '[*Twilight*] is far from perfect: Edward's portrayal as monstrous tragic hero is overly Byronic, and Bella's appeal is based on magic rather than character,' it wrote. 'Nonetheless, the portrayal of dangerous lovers hits the spot; fans of dark romance will find it hard to resist.'

It wasn't just the critics who loved it: readers did too, rushing out in their droves to buy this strange new tale of passion and thwarted love. Soon *Twilight* began to win prizes: the *New York Times* named it as Editor's Choice, it was one of *Publishers Weekly*'s top children's books (although in truth, the readership contained almost as many adults as it did teens), and it made the American Library Association's Top-Ten Best Books For Young Adults and Top-Ten Books For Reluctant Readers. No one was in any doubt that the publishers had a smash hit on their hands.

The comparisons with J. K. Rowling began, and Stephenie, very wisely, embraced them, at the same time acknowledging her debt to the writer who had gone before.

'I'm a big fan,' she told *The Times*. 'All of us YA [young adult] writers are, especially those of us who write big books. If it weren't for her, our books wouldn't even have gotten a chance. People wouldn't put an 800-page YA book on the shelf because there was no way kids were going to read it. Now everyone knows that kids love big books, you just have to make them interesting for them. Everyone is looking for the next J. K. Rowling. It's not going to happen. That's just something that is never going to happen again. She was, is, something that will not be repeated.' But Stephenie was coming remarkably close.

In 2006, the next book in the series appeared: *New Moon*, a reference to the darkest phase of the lunar cycle, mirroring the darkest phase of Bella's life. It kicks off with Bella's growing realization that she will grow old and Edward will not, when she has a dream in which she sees herself as an old woman with Edward, still her devoted lover and still seventeen, at her side. This is rubbed in by the fact that it is now her birthday, and she is eighteen – a year older than Edward.

The Cullens have prepared a birthday party for her, but almost immediately it starts to go wrong. As she opens her presents, she gives herself a paper cut: a spot of blood appears on her finger, which sends Jasper into a frenzy of bloodlust. He attacks her: as Edward intervenes, Bella falls onto a glass table, from which she is even more badly cut. Only Carlisle Cullen, the father of the household, and a doctor whose work in hospitals has given him almost supernatural self-control in the presence of blood, can cope: he bandages Bella up and gets her home safely.

The incident, however, makes Edward realize that simply spending time with the Cullens is terribly dangerous for Bella, and so, in a supreme act of self-sacrifice, he tells Bella he doesn't want her anymore and leaves town, along with the rest of his family. Bella falls into a terrible depression from which it takes her months to emerge, and even then, she's barely capable of functioning. It is only when her father threatens to send her home to her mother that Bella attempts some semblance of the life she had before.

With Bella having neglected absolutely everyone for months, her school 'friend' Jessica is both surprised and mistrustful when Bella suggests they go to see a movie. Matters do not improve when, after the film, Bella passes a bar with shady-looking men hanging out in the doorway, and approaches them as they remind her of one of the numerous occasions when Edward saved her life. She hears Edward's voice in her head, warning her not to be so foolish, from which point it begins to appear whenever she's in trouble. This is not a spur towards being sensible.

Bella decides that if she can't have Edward, at least she can hear him, and so buys a couple of run-down motorbikes – the perfect dangerous vehicles – which she gets her friend Jacob Black to restore. Concurrently, she sees people on the reservation jumping off cliffs into the sea for sport: Bella, too, decides to do this and Jacob agrees to help her one day.

However, something strange is beginning to happen to Jacob. He had been frightened by the fact that his friends appeared to be joining an ominous gang headed by the seemingly sinister Sam Uley, but now he drifts in that direction, too, refusing to meet Bella. When she attempts to see him, she is told he is ill. However, Bella perseveres, finally breaking through to him – and discovering that he has turned into the sworn enemy of the vampire: a werewolf.

Werewolves are only called into being when there is danger from a vampire, and this soon proves to be the case. Victoria – a member of the vampire coven that attempted to kill Bella in the first book, and the partner of James, the vampire who was destroyed – is back and looking to wreak vengeance. A spate of human killings has begun.

Bella, meanwhile, desperate to hear Edward's voice, is becoming increasingly reckless, and plunges off the cliffs into the sea on her own, unaware that a storm is brewing. She nearly drowns, but is rescued at the last minute by Jacob.

Slowly, Bella realizes she has feelings for Jacob, as he certainly does for her, but she equally appreciates that Edward will always be the only one for her. On returning home, she finds Alice Cullen: her first contact for months with the family she so adores. Alice had had a vision of Bella hurtling into the sea, but because vampires cannot see the future of werewolves, she was unaware that Jacob saved her, and thought her friend had drowned. Enormously relieved that Bella is still alive, Alice is nonetheless shocked by her obvious suffering, and tells her that Edward, too, has been in pain.

On the day of Bella's jump, Charlie's friend Harry Clearwater dies, leading to a mix-up that almost ends in a *Romeo and Juliet* scenario. Jacob is at the house when the phone rings and he tells the caller that Charlie is 'at the funeral'. The caller, though Bella doesn't yet realize it, was Edward, and having heard of Alice's vision via his sister Rosalie, he assumes the funeral referred to is Bella's. Consumed by grief, he decides to commit suicide. He plans to do this by going to Volterra in Italy, home of the Volturi, a very ancient coven of vampires who are essentially the law enforcers of the vampire world. He decides to expose his skin to the sun there. The Volturi would never allow him to do this, naturally, as it would expose their vampiric secret to the world: they would destroy him first, which is just what Edward has in mind.

With the clock ticking, Alice and Bella speed to Volterra to show Edward she is still alive: they get to him just in time, but they are all captured and taken deep into the Volturi lair. The Volturi realize, of course, that Bella, a human, now knows about the existence of vampires, and they give Edward an ultimatum: she must become one herself or pay with her life.

This transformation is, in fact, what Bella now wants, and after they have been allowed to return to Forks, she asks the rest of the Cullens if they will help her to make the transition. Carlisle appears to give a cautious yes. Edward, however, cannot countenance the idea. However, realizing how determined Bella is to go through with it, he offers her a deal: he will change her himself if she marries him. (Bella has an aversion to the idea of marriage in the wake of her parents' divorce, and so Edward hopes to buy a little more time for the human Bella through this negotiation.) The book ends with nothing resolved.

Like its predecessor, *New Moon* was an immediate sensation. It went straight into the *New York Times* bestseller list for children's books, in its second week rising to the number-one slot, and spent a total of thirty weeks on the list. The reviews were also positive: 'Less streamlined than *Twilight* yet just as exciting, *New Moon* will more than feed the bloodthirsty hankerings of fans of the first volume and leave them breathless for the third,' wrote Hillias J. Martin in *School Library Journal*.

There was also a critique on Teenreads.com: 'In the middle, the story sometimes drags, and readers may long for the vampires' return,' it read. 'The events of *New Moon*, though, will leave Meyer's many fans breathless for the sequel, as Bella finally understands everything that will be at stake if she makes the ultimate choice to give up her humanity and live, like the vampires, forever.'

New Moon was, in fact, slightly unusual, in that Edward appears only at the beginning and the end. It is Jacob who is the central male figure throughout most of the book, although he is dismissed when Bella is reunited with her great love. This had the effect of creating an alternative heart-throb, both in the character of Jacob in the books, and in the actor who went on to play him, Taylor Lautner. There began to emerge a strong fan base for both men: the Edward aficionados and the Jacob brigade. Rob, as Edward, did have a rival – although there was no question that ultimately he always had the edge.

The narrative of *New Moon*, while limited in terms of the screen time it would eventually offer Rob, was nevertheless packed full of stimulating dramatic opportunities. The self-sacrifice in the early part of the book was a case in point. Edward must convincingly 'act' his cool dismissal of Bella, but all the time, inside, he would be near to self-destruction. That would undoubtedly be a compli-cated dynamic to portray.

Moreover, the suicidal scenes in Volterra were an actor's gift. Though comedy can be fun to film, many thespians find that they appreciate the darker narratives of scripts more, both emotionally and dramatically. Judging by Rob's catalogue of work, he was just such an actor. He had already, to a lesser degree, toyed with dramatizing depression and alienation in his role in *How to Be*. The psychological disarray he had demonstrated to such critical acclaim in *The Haunted Airman*, meanwhile, gave a promising taster of how these movie scenes might unfold.

After all, this was the most nightmarish scenario yet for Edward: the pinnacle of his self-loathing, the loss of hope in the face of Bella's perceived demise, and the soulless expectation of what he thought would follow his death. At the time of writing, *New Moon* the film has not yet been released, but all the signs are there that Rob will pull off something pretty spectacular for the movie's calamitous climax.

The next book, *Eclipse*, the third in the quartet, came out a year after *New Moon*, with a publication date of 7 August 2007. By now the print run was approaching *Potter*-esque proportions, with a hardback release of 1 million copies: this soon turned out to be justified, as the book sold more than 150,000 copies in the first twenty-four hours of its release.

In *Eclipse*, Edward was firmly back at the centre of the action, which is where he was to remain from now on. The book opens with a series of unsolved murders, which Edward realizes are vampire attacks. He and Bella have other things on their minds, however: both are applying to college; Bella wants to see Jacob again, which is difficult because, as a werewolf, he is a sworn enemy of the vampires; and Alice has had a vision that Victoria, the vicious vampire, has returned to Forks. In the middle of all of this, Bella eventually accepts Edward's offer of marriage and transformation.

Soon it becomes clear that Victoria is behind the murders: she has assembled an army of 'newborn' vampires, and they have gone on the rampage. In order to combat this, old enmities are overcome, and the Cullens join forces with the werewolves to fight off this new threat. Edward, Bella and Jacob retreat to the mountains, where they are joined by another young werewolf, Seth Clearwater. Matters are disturbed when Jacob, who has long been in love with Bella, hears her discussing her engagement to Edward. Distraught, he says he will join the battle. Bella kisses him to stop him from leaving, and in doing so, realizes she loves him, too.

Victoria, meanwhile, has managed to isolate Edward's scent, and tracks the quartet into the mountains, where she forces Edward to fight to defend himself and the others. She and her army of new vampires are ultimately destroyed. And now Bella must make her choice: between Edward and Jacob – inevitably, perhaps, she chooses the former. Rather tactlessly, the two of them invite Jacob to their wedding: he turns back into a wolf and runs off, only able to keep his pain at bay when in his animal form.

The pictures on all the four covers of the books have a meaning, and so it was in this case, too. The *Eclipse* cover shows a torn red ribbon, which, Stephenie has explained, represents choice. Bella must choose between Edward and Jacob, while the ribbon also portrays the idea that Bella can never fully escape her human life: a part of her will always be tied to it.

By the time *Eclipse* was published, it was apparent that here was a phenomenon in the making, and so this time around publication was marked by the type of events that were previously associated with the *Harry Potter* books. A couple of months before the book came out, Stephenie was called upon to host an '*Eclipse* Prom' at Arizona State University; the tickets sold out in seven hours. A second prom was announced on the same day: this time the tickets took four hours to sell out. Stephenie also posted regular teasers for readers on her website, and in the thirty-seven days leading up to publication, an exclusive quote was posted from the new book each day.

On the whole, the reviews were positive, although there were a couple of sour notes that foreshadowed what was to be said about the fourth and final book. 'Meyer knows what her fans want: thrills, chills, and a lot of romance, and she delivers on all counts,' wrote Anne Rouyer of *School Library Journal*. Selby Gibson-Boyce of *Tulsa World* explained, 'I read without stopping until I finished. Meyer's book would not detach itself from my hand. Exactly the same thing happened with *Twilight* and *New Moon*.'

Kellan Rice of *Blast* magazine was not so keen. She lambasted the book as sexist: 'Not only does Meyer give her two characters an obviously unhealthy – even abusive – relationship, but she romanticizes and idealizes it, and not only with Bella and Edward, but with Bella and Jacob as well.' It was a foretaste of what was to come the next year.

In 2008, the fourth and, to date, final book of the series was published: *Breaking Dawn*. Launch date was 2 August and it was clear to all concerned that publication was going to be a huge event. Many bookshops in the United States held special midnight-release parties, just as they had done with the *Potter* books in earlier years. So buoyed up was interest in the proceedings that the print run was 3.7 million hardback copies. Of these, 1.3 million sold in the first twenty-four hours, setting a record.

Yet the critical reaction to *Breaking Dawn* was to be far more mixed than Meyer had ever received before, even if, for fans, the final union of Edward and Bella, and Bella's transformation into a vampire was exactly what they wanted. The title refers to this transition and Bella's new life, and the cover is again highly symbolic: it shows a chess board with a white queen in the foreground and a red pawn in the background. The message is that Bella has moved from being pawn to queen.

Breaking Dawn opens with Bella and Edward's wedding and their honeymoon on a remote island off the coast of Brazil where, finally, they consummate their relationship (Stephenie's Mormon beliefs would make this acceptable, as they are now legally wed). Bella becomes pregnant; a pregnancy that appears to be proceeding extremely quickly, leading Edward to become concerned that they have bred a monster, upon which he urges Bella to have an abortion. She refuses and the pregnancy continues.

At this point, the narrative switches to Jacob's perspective, which is where it stays until Bella has given birth. The werewolf pack discovers Bella is pregnant and decides it must destroy the unborn child, in the process killing Bella, too. Jacob will have none of it and leaves to form a new pack, taking Leah and Seth Clearwater with him. At this point, Bella goes into labour and, in one of the most controversial scenes in the book, is nearly destroyed in the process, as almost all her bones are broken and she loses a huge amount of blood. As she nears death, Edward finally grants her wish and does the only thing he can to save her, transforming her into a vampire.

Here, the narrative returns to Bella herself. Naming their baby Renesmee, she and Edward are initially happy in their new life, until another vampire, Irina, wrongly identifies Renesmee as an 'immortal child' – in other words, a vampire child, uncontrollable and outlawed by the Volturi. The child, and the Cullens, are thus set to be destroyed by the vampire law enforcers.

The Cullens call on their vampire friends from all over the world to testify that Renesmee is *not* an immortal child, and the scene is set for a confrontation between the Volturi and the Cullens and their allies. The Volturi are the type to torture first and ask questions later, but fate intervenes. Now that she, too, is a vampire, Bella, like some of the others, finds that she has a superpower that ultimately enables her to save the vampires from destroying one another. Even when she was human, Edward was unable to read her mind, while the psychological powers that others exerted could also not harm her. Now, she is able to extend that protection to everyone else, and keep the Volturi at bay until the Cullens have presented their case.

When the Volturi eventually realize their mistake about the nature of Renesmee's existence, they execute Irina for lying to them. A problem remains, though, in that Renesmee will know of the existence of vampires, and there is much debate about what to do about that, until Alice and Jasper, hitherto absent, appear on the scene. With them is Nahuel, like Renesmee the product of a human/vampire relationship, 150 years old and no threat to the vampire community. After seeing him, the Volturi leave and the new family is left to live in peace.

It was in many ways the only satisfactory ending to the tale. Not only does Bella get her prince, or rather, vampire, but she and Edward can now be bound together in eternity – and remain the same age. However, the critics were outraged, especially those who felt that women are far better off forging a career, rather than marrying vampires and having strange, half-vampiric children. 'Essentially, everyone gets everything they want, even if their desires necessitate an about-face in characterization or the messy introduction of some back story,' snorted *Publishers Weekly*. 'Nobody has to renounce anything or suffer more than temporarily – in other words, grandeur is out.'

The Independent wasn't any happier: the book was 'shockingly, tackily, sick-makingly sexist', adding for good measure that 'Bella Swan lives to serve men and suffer'. The *Washington Post* said,

'Meyer has put a stake through the heart of her own beloved creation,' adding, '*Breaking Dawn* has a childbirth sequence that may promote lifelong abstinence in sensitive types.' *Entertainment Weekly* also slated the birth scene, along with Bella's passion for Edward. And so on.

Stephenie Meyer, who had been laughing all the way to the bank for some years now, was utterly unperturbed. The book was suffering from the 'Rob effect', she said – just as the fans had needed some time to accept Rob as their hero, so they needed space to come to terms with the end of the book. And there was a considerably cheerier reaction from elsewhere. The book won the British Book Award Children's Book of the Year, beating off competition from J. K. Rowling's *The Tales of Beedle the Bard*, and in 2009, in the Children's Choice Book Awards, the novel was chosen as Teen Choice Book of the Year, while Meyer was named Author of the Year. If she was upset by the reviews, then she was hiding it awfully well.

And while the critics might have loathed it, the fans felt the opposite. Bella (and so in their imagination, themselves) had achieved the impossible and found true love. Many were also keen to point out – as did Rob himself when the film-making of *Twilight* began – that it was Bella, not Edward, who saved the day. So could it really be slated as an anti-feminist tract?

There is one oddity about *Breaking Dawn*, however, and that is that, unlike the other novels, it is not necessarily going to be made into a film. The producers have given the project the go-ahead, but there are several obstacles ahead. The first is that Stephenie herself has said that the book is so long, it would have to be two films rather than one. The second is that Renesmee would be very difficult to portray, for although she is a baby, she has full intellectual awareness.

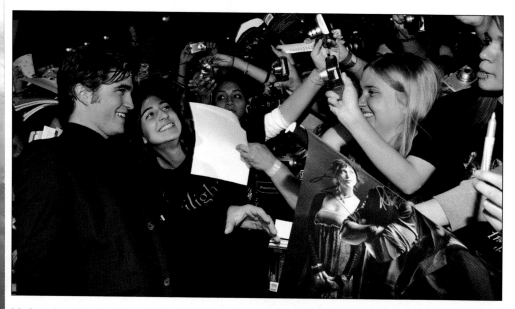

It's fangdemonium: Rob meets and greets fans at the *Twilight* premiere in LA.

I only have eyes for you?
Rumours abound about
the true nature of Rob and
Kristen's close friendship.

On the red carpet in LA with (from left to right) his co-stars
Nikki Reed and Kristen Stewart, and director Catherine
Hardwicke.

Overleaf: To promote *Twilight*,
the two actors starred in this
stunning photo shoot with
Vanity Fair.

Rob as Edward Cullen.

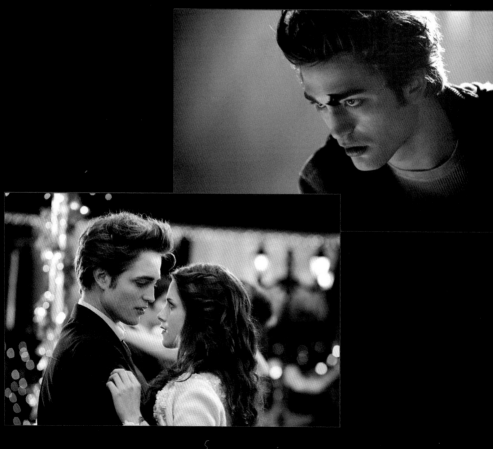

Twilight was a worldwide smash – and demanded a global tour from its stars. Here Rob is hard at work in Paris (above), Tokyo (left, with Kristen and Taylor) and Rome (below).

Hollywood hero: at the 2009 Oscars (above).

Will they or won't they? Rob and Kristen keep fans guessing as they collect their MTV Movie Award for Best Kiss (below).

Hanging on his every word: Rob – and the world's media – at the 2009 Cannes Film Festival.

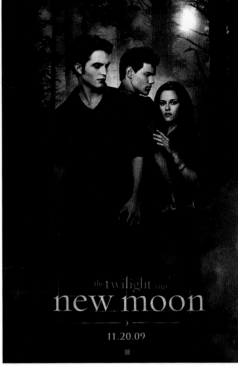

Mobbed in the street: Rob tries to film *Remember Me* in New York.

The poster for the second *Twilight* film, *New Moon*.

Forbidden love: a heart-stopping still from *New Moon*.

And there is a third dilemma. If a film does go ahead, Rob would not necessarily be in it. He was signed up for three films, not four. Could they really make *Breaking Dawn* without the leading man who has set the world on fire? Could the fans stomach anyone other than Rob as Edward?

eight
edward unbound

July 7 2007. Stephenie Meyer, author of one of the most success-ful series of books that has ever been published, had just posted a blog on her website. 'I am very excited to announce that *Twilight* has been optioned by Summit Entertainment,' she wrote. 'The people at Summit seem quite enthusiastic about doing *Twilight* the right way, and I'm looking forward to working with them. The story will be optioned for the next fifteen months.'

This was not, in fact, the first time Stephenie had been in talks over making a film of the books: she had previously been in negoti-ations with MTV Film, but nothing had come of it. However, it was clear that a movie based on the first book of her bestselling quartet would be a smash hit – for a start, its filmic qualities were apparent practically from the first page. The greeny grey landscape of Forks, the statuesque Cullen family, the vampiric skin that glittered when the sun came out – it all betokened a runaway success ... and so it was to prove to be.

Of course, there was intense interest in the casting from the word go, not least from Stephenie herself. Her first choice for the role of Edward had actually been the actor Henry Cavill, whose breakthrough role had been in *I Capture the Castle* and who, funnily enough, had also been considered for the role of Cedric

Diggory, but talks about the film had been going on for some years now, and Henry had reached the grand old age of twenty-four, making him too old for the part. It would have to be somebody else.

But who? Stephenie kept up an active dialogue with her fans via the website, and so she posted her own suggestions, along with inviting those from the readers. There were various stipulations about who would play Edward: he had to be twenty-one or under, and he couldn't be a model or a singer in a band. He had to be a real actor.

Early names in the fray were Tom Sturridge (who bears a slight resemblance to Rob, and is in fact a good friend of his) and Logan Lerman. Tyler Posey was a suggestion for Jacob, with Emily Browning a possible for Bella. Stephenie also felt that Charlie Hunnam might do for Carlisle, with John C. Reilly, or perhaps Vince Vaughn, as Charlie. Other thoughts were Rachel Leigh Cook as Alice, Cillian Murphy for James, Daniel Cudmore as Emmett, Joanna Krupa as Rosalie (Stephenie was breaking her own rules here, as Joanna is a model), John Stamos as Laurent and Graham Greene for Billy.

The fans responded in their droves and Stephenie published some of their choices, by order of popularity, online. Amazingly, given the fuss some fans made when he actually did get chosen, Rob was on the list: it went, in order, Hayden Christensen, Rob, Orlando Bloom and Gerard Way. Stephenie's own next suggestions for Edward, which she quite shamelessly admitted were based on looks rather than anything else, were Mike Vogel, Drew Fuller, Hugh Dancy and Jackson Rathbone.

For Bella, the fans wanted Alexis Bledel, Rachel McAdams and Anna Paquin; Stephenie was mulling over Danielle Panabaker.

Fans wanted Trent Ford or Calum Best as Jasper; they were also nominating Dennis Quaid as Charlie, Olivia Wilde as Rosalie and either Mary-Louise Parker or Jean Louise Kelly as Esme. When casting was finally complete, only two names remained from those early days: Rob Pattinson, and Jackson Rathbone, who would eventually be cast as Jasper.

Edward was a role to die for, as it were, and behind the scenes intensive competition was going on among actors who wanted the part. Again, as with the role of Harry Potter, it was a certainty that whoever got the part of Edward was going to turn into a huge star: this was the kind of opportunity that could be the making of a career. And funnily enough, the choice was not at all an obvious one.

Although Edward was an American vampire, Rob himself revealed that Stephenie wanted a Brit. 'It's weird because there were a lot of British people up for this part,' he said on atwilight-kiss.com. 'The author's choice was an English guy, which was really strange. She wanted all English guys to play Americans. I think there is something about this myth in America of British people being classy.'

There was another element, too: the Cullens are outsiders in Forks, unable to mix fully with the rest of the townsfolk. Stephenie might have felt that non-American actors would be able to portray this sense of otherness better, although in the end Rob was the only Englishman to get a part in the film.

By the end of August 2007, things were really coming together. Catherine Hardwicke had been signed up as the film's director, and Melissa Rosenberg as the writer, with Catherine visiting Forks shortly after her appointment to get a feel for the twilit town and its haunting surrounds. In the wake of the books and the films, it was to become a tourist destination for fans.

The first major casting announcement came in November – on the 16th, to be exact – with the news that Kristen Stewart was to play the role of Bella. 'We at Summit are truly excited about the franchise potential of this remarkable *Romeo and Juliet* story,' said Erik Feig, Summit Entertainment's President of Production. 'Of course, you are only as good as your Juliet and Kristen Stewart has that magical combination of being a great actress, deeply appealing and perfect for the part.'

Kristen was not a newcomer to film: in fact, she had far more experience than Rob. Born 9 April 1990, Kristen had appeared in her first film, *The Safety of Objects*, at the tender age of eleven, and had had her breakthrough role just one year later, in *Panic Room*, starring opposite Jodie Foster. Over ten films followed over the next few years, including *Zathura: A Space Adventure* and *In the Land of Women*; by now, she was a real pro.

Less than a month later, the announcement everyone was waiting for came through. 'Summit Entertainment announced today that Robert Pattinson will star as Edward in the highly anticipated feature film production *Twilight* opposite Kristen Stewart,' announced the *Los Angeles Times*. 'The thriller-romance, based on Stephenie Meyer's publishing phenomenon, is slated to begin production in February 2008 with Catherine Hardwicke directing a script by Melissa Rosenberg.'

Erik Feig chipped in again: 'It is always a challenge to find the right actor for a part that has lived so vividly in the imaginations of readers, but we took the responsibility seriously and are confident, with Rob Pattinson, that we have found the perfect Edward for our Bella in *Twilight*,' he said. The announcements about the rest of the cast followed in due course.

Rob himself had been extremely diffident about going up for

the part. He has about him a genuine modesty and shyness, and the emphasis in the book on Edward's physical perfection is such that he admitted he felt something of a fraud even to consider the part. When VanityFair.com asked him if he'd wanted it, he replied, 'Somewhat, but I was literally embarrassed walking into the audition. I had no idea how to play Edward at all. I thought that even going into the audition was completely pointless, because they were just going to cast a model or something. I felt it was kind of arrogant of me to even go in. I was almost having a full-on panic attack before I went to the screen test.'

Indeed, he was later to admit that his nerves were such that he took a small amount of Valium to keep himself calm. Betraying a vulnerability which was to reappear when he spoke of his amazement at the hysteria he provoked among fans, he confessed in an interview with *GQ* magazine: 'I took half a Valium and then went into this thing [the audition] – and all this stuff happened. It was the first time I've ever taken Valium. A quarter. A quarter of a Valium. I tried to do it for another audition, and it just completely backfired – I was passing out.'

Until he heard about the role, Rob had not even read the book. 'I read the book like five months before casting. I read the first fifty pages, up until when he gets introduced and I was just like, "No." Because I was really fat last year as well,' he told film.com. 'So it was just like embarrassing. I thought the whole thing was embarrassing, even turning up to the audition. I hadn't read the whole book before the audition, but even the four-line synopsis – "Edward is the perfect being. He's so witty and beautiful. He's crazy and funny. He'll open doors for you. He'll drive you in his Volvo" – I thought even turning up would be embarrassing.'

It was this attitude, though, that was crucial to Rob being so suited to the role. Had he turned up to the audition and behaved as if he thought he was God's gift, then such conceit and smirking self-awareness would have been utterly at odds with the slightly alienated figure of Edward. As it was, his point-blank refusal to accept that there was anything special about himself chimed in with Edward's occasional self-loathing. Unwittingly, his approach helped him to get the part.

Kristen, of course, had already been chosen for the role of Bella, and she had some say about who would be playing opposite her. It was absolutely essential that the two leads got on, on-screen at least (in fact, rumours were later to grow about their off-screen relationship, too, of which more anon), and had she felt that Rob was not the man for the job, chances are he would still be living in Soho making art-house films that never got released. Happily, and understandably, she thought he was perfect for the part. 'Everybody came in doing something empty and shallow and thoughtless,' said Kristen, who was one of Rob's leading champions. 'Rob understood that it wasn't a frivolous role.'

But it couldn't be awarded on Kristen's say-so alone. The importance of the chemistry between Edward and Bella, or Rob and Kristen, cannot be overestimated. By the time the film's makers had narrowed it down to the last five, it was critical they got it right, as the film's director Catherine Hardwicke made clear. 'So we had like four different finalists came over, and then Robert came over,' she told atwilightkiss.com. 'Each of them tried different scenes – three different scenes with Kristen. And so for the bedroom scenes, yeah, we went into the bedroom [of my funky beach house]. I'm just there with the camera and kind of feeling the magic sort of come alive. And that chemistry, it was pretty exciting.'

And so the announcement was made: Summit had found its Edward. The reaction from the fans was immediate – and apoplectic with rage. *Harry Potter and the Goblet of Fire* apart, Rob's choice of films and roles seemed a little odd for someone who was to play a character that was such a heart-throb, while he himself appeared to be as bemused as anyone else that he'd got the role. There was a roar of fury that seemed to echo from coast to coast – something that Rob's own mother pointed out to him, albeit with no intention of hurting the feelings of her soon-to-be stratospherically famous son.

'My mum sent me some stuff, which she thought was really funny, when I was already in America,' Rob told film.com. 'They had this picture from this Viking film I did, where I looked like someone had beaten me in the face with a frying pan. I was wearing this disgusting wig. And they were like: "*This* is Edward." It was a petition, which they were going to send to Summit, saying, "We will not go and see the movie." It got up to 75,000 signings. This is about three days after I got cast. I was thinking, "Thanks for sending that, Mum!" That was my welcome into *Twilight*.' The *Nibelungs* had come back to haunt him.

So had *Harry Potter*. While it was certainly not impossible to be a fan of both series of books and films, followers of each liked to think they were unique. To have a crossover from one to the other just wasn't on. Worse still, the slightly buttoned-up character of the English Cedric was nothing at all like the tortured and American Edward. How could one person possibly play both roles? Rob, sensibly, kept his head down and didn't rise to the bait. 'The books have a huge following, and I've already got bags of letters from angry fans telling me that I can't possibly play Edward because I'm Diggory,' he said in an interview with *ES* magazine. 'I hope I can prove them wrong.'

He made light of it all, but it was an exceedingly hurtful, albeit short-lived, time in his life. It is one thing to disparage your own looks; quite another when other people do it for you. Stephenie was concerned about him, as were the film's producers: after all, he was still a very young man, only twenty-one, and he was having to carry not only the massive expectations for the film on his shoulders, as one of the leading actors, but all the weight of this negativity, too. It was not exactly conducive to building confidence in himself, and it was briefly a matter of real concern.

But the die – like the role of Edward – was cast: there was no going back now. Rob had moved to the States for the audition: he was now to be based in LA on a semi-permanent basis, as the huge production machine behind *Twilight* started to roll. Filming, which was set to last for six months, was not due to begin until the new year (although Rob had now been cast, some of the other roles still needed to be filled), but work off-screen started right away – namely, with a personal trainer. The role of Edward was necessarily going to involve some bare-chested scenes, and the *Twilight* bosses wanted the pecs that a superhumanly strong vampire should have to be on display.

There followed a very intensive few months of working out. When he was asked what he would be doing to distract himself during the long hours on set, he told *ES* magazine: 'I hope I'll have the courage not to take anything with me at all. I want to be a bit monkish about it and focus completely on the work. I'll try to get up each morning at 5.30 to go running.' Rob was certainly dedicated.

And it wasn't long before the fans changed their minds. After Stephenie had given Rob her public endorsement, famously saying, 'I am ecstatic with Summit's choice for Edward. There are very few actors who can look both beautiful and dangerous at the same time, and even fewer who I can picture in my head as Edward. Robert Pattinson is going to be amazing,' the climate began to change. A few more recent pictures of Rob were published: far from being the Viking with the bad haircut, here was an astoundingly handsome young man, all cheekbones and razor-sharp jawline, with an amazing ruffle of unruly hair.

That hair alone was to become the subject of heated debate, with Rob being told not to cut it. Nor, according to the man himself, did he wash it. A couple of months later, he said as much during an appearance on *The Tonight Show with Jay Leno*; the model Heidi Klum, also in situ, rather nervously moved away.

Another skill Rob had to learn was the US sport of baseball. The vampire baseball game, which takes place in a clearing deep in the woods, is a central scene within the book and the film: it alerts the evil coven of visiting vampires to the fact that the Cullens are harbouring a human in their midst, and sets off the terrifying chase in which James, the tracker vampire, goes in pursuit of Bella. In the film, the vampires' superspeed makes for some breathtaking special effects. However, there's only so much the computers can do, and all the actors were required to develop a good standard of play, which the special effects would later embellish. Having been brought up in Britain, however, Rob hadn't a clue how to play the game, and so was forced to learn this, too, before the cameras started to roll.

Rob and the subject of baseball caused a great deal of amusement in the United States: it was the equivalent of a young American actor coming to Britain and having to learn to play cricket. At least in the *Harry Potter* films no one had teased him about not being able to play Quidditch; this was quite something else, though, as he ruefully observed.

'I've been asked this everywhere,' he told film.com. '"So I understand you're crap at baseball?" I just didn't care. I think sports are stupid. Catherine Hardwicke was so determined to make me look like a professional baseball player. She had this coach trying to teach me the "ready" position, like a little squat. I was like, "Seriously, I'll do it on the day. You don't have to teach me." But Catherine wanted to see it, in front of all these extras. It was just very embarrassing. So for the rest of the shoot, whenever Catherine couldn't decide how to block a shot, I'd say, "I think I should be doing my ready position." But yeah, I'm terrible at baseball. I'm terrible at every sport apart from running, but I'm terrible at that now, too.'

Rob was, as usual, being self-effacing. He was actually a very accomplished sportsman, as witnessed previously on the set of *Harry Potter*, and in evidence again now. Certainly, no one watching his athletic displays in *Twilight* – both on the baseball field and as he dominates the forest landscape of Forks – would describe his efforts as 'terrible'.

By February 2008, casting was complete. Peter Facinelli was to portray Carlisle; Elizabeth Reaser, Esme; Jackson Rathbone, Jasper; Nikki Reed, Rosalie; Ashley Greene, Alice; and Kellan Lutz, Emmett. Other major cast members included Billy Burke as Charlie, Rachelle Lefevre as Victoria and, of course, Taylor Lautner as Jacob Black.

Utterly different from Rob physically – in that he comes across as an all-American muscled jock, in comparison to Rob's wiry, perhaps more European frame; with dark features a testimony to his Native American heritage (in fact, Taylor also has French, Dutch and German blood in his veins) as opposed to Rob's pale complexion – Taylor was to become a serious rival in the heart-throb stakes, building up a huge fan base of his own. Like Kristen, although he was only sixteen when he was cast for *Twilight*, he was also an experienced film actor, with roles in, amongst much else, *The Adventures of Sharkboy and Lavagirl in 3-D* and *Cheaper by the Dozen 2* to his name.

In the months that followed, as filming began, there was really fierce interest in how it progressed. This was not an easy role to play: much as Edward was utterly desirable, take the intensity too far and it could all go completely over the top. Rob was clearly terrified of looking like a prat, as he confessed once filming had got underway, and his old preoccupation with Edward's famed beauty was also clearly on his mind.

'I basically spent two months thinking, "OK, how can I play this character like he is written and be absolutely nothing like him in real life?"' he told VanityFair.com. '"How can I get away from the most major aspect of his description – his appearance?" As it is written from Bella's perspective, she describes him in this obsessively lustful way. She does not see a single flaw in him at all. It's a very traditional aspect of first or young love. So, it took me ages to think of it, but it ended up being really simple: if you are in love with someone, you can't see any flaw in the other person. So I finally figured out that I didn't have to play the most beautiful man on the planet, but just play a man in love.'

The fans weren't the only ones fascinated by the process. Stephenie Meyer (like J. K. Rowling) was taking a very active interest in how her stories transferred to the screen. She had been on set a few times by now, watching what her characters were getting up to, and had even been in front of the camera, in a cameo role as an extra. (You can spot her as a customer at the bar in the diner, in a scene where Bella and Charlie are having dinner.) These experiences were gleefully related on her blog.

'My favourite part was dinner with some of the cast and crew,' she wrote. 'You don't know surreal until you sit down at a table with people out of your imagination. It was more than a little bit disturbing how pretty everyone was – and who knew movie stars were so nice? Anyway, if you ever get a chance to visit the set of a movie based on a book you wrote, I definitely recommend that you go for it.' Her happiness at seeing her creation turned into something visible, as opposed to merely readable, was palpable.

She and the young stars were very pleased with how it was all progressing. She gave them a few tips, too. In fact, this was a big opportunity for them to understand the rationale behind their characters better – and share it with the fans, as well. 'The main thing I asked her is why Edward has accepted Carlisle as he has,' revealed Rob to MTV News. 'He sometimes treats him as his father and sometimes as a sort of partner. I was just wondering why this 108-year-old guy would pretend to be a seventeen-year-old boy to someone who knows that he's not seventeen.

'And she said that Edward has judged Carlisle to be a good enough person to deserve him acting like his son – which I thought was very interesting. It's a very, very strange thing to do, if you have absolutely no relation to someone, and [to keep up the charade], just because they've stolen your soul against your will. Edward has found it within himself to forgive him to such an extent. [...] There aren't many scenes that show that, but I thought it was an interesting dynamic.'

That reference to stealing the soul was of paramount importance: because Edward feels that he has no soul, there is a kind of existential despair about him that lifts only when he meets Bella. She gives him, literally, a reason to live.

Consequently, Rob believed that the character of Bella was

crucial to understanding the role of Edward. 'The more Bella says, "I'm not scared of you, you're not a monster," the more Edward believes it himself, and he forgets that he is a vampire and what his actual urges are,' he explained to www.teenhollywood.com. 'He tries to kiss her and, obviously, it ends up being a nightmare. She has this hormonal rush, and I have the "I want to kill you" [rush]. It ends up being quite sexy, in a weird way. You're at a point where you want to do everything and kill them, at the same time. It's the peak.'

Kristen, on the other hand, took a very different approach to meeting the author: she was less interested in Bella's motivation and more concerned about how the books came about. 'Me and Stephenie got along pretty well,' she said. 'She's a warm person. But I didn't speak to her about my character or the books. I asked her how she got to write them and what other kinds of books she likes and stuff like that, but I didn't talk about the story.'

Rob was asked for his take on the role, and the character itself. He provided a very revealing portrait as to how he saw Edward, and how he interpreted the role. Whether or not he realized it, Rob was creating an intensely romantic figure: a man who is ultimately defined by his love for a woman. But this love can never be straightforward, because the desire to be with her is so strongly connected with the desire to kill her. As a devout Mormon, Stephenie might not have realized she was exploring so openly the link between sex and death – the subject of fascination for many a writer before her – but she was, and Rob understood that.

'He's a semi-reluctant vampire, who doesn't really know why he even exists,' he told www.agirlsworld.com. 'He's always thinking, "I either want to die, or become a human because just being a vampire is so utterly pointless." He's 108 years old, maybe 109.

He's stuck in the body of a seventeen-year-old schoolkid, pretending to be a human. And then, he finds this mortal girl, Bella, and initially wants to devour her. Then, it turns into an all-consuming love for her. It's just very difficult for a vampire to be in love with someone he wants to eat all the time. The story is the problems, the trials and the tribulations which occur when a vampire falls in love with a normal girl that he wants to kill.'

As well as analysing Edward's character, Rob also had to think about vampires themselves. In interviews, he was often asked if he'd done much research into vampiric lore. After all, tales of these beings, who would visit humans in the dark hours and suck out their life blood, had been around for thousands of years, so there existed a vast canon that Rob could have called upon for research. There was naturally some curiosity as to whether Rob had looked to these age-old creatures for inspiration, be it in books or in their more modern interpretations in recent films and TV series.

'[I didn't do research] on vampires really,' said Robert to www. teenhollywood.com. 'I guess it's kind of easy to make it clichéd. There're so many hundreds of thousands of vampire movies.' And Rob was also aware that the *Twilight* vampires were somewhat different. 'In the story, they're not really conventional vampires. They don't really look like vampires, and they don't die in the sun. Every little characteristic of vampires is just abandoned. I was trying to do it in as basic a way as possible. You just get bitten by somebody, and then you're a vampire and you live forever, and you're superstrong and stuff.'

It was a light-hearted response, but it was central to Rob's portrayal of Edward because, as he explained at other times, he didn't exactly play Edward as a vampire, but rather as a man in love who happens to be a vampire. Had he concentrated more on the notion of, say, the 'undead' than the central romance, his interpretation would not have worked anything like as well.

As usual, Rob's instincts were right. Though vampires are traditionally the stuff of nightmares, many of them in the *Twilight* series are deeply sympathetic figures, condemned to an existence they didn't necessarily want. As Rob saw it, their plight is heightened by the fact that they were once human themselves, and know what it is they've turned into. They exist in a world they were once part of, but can never now go back to, nor live as they once did.

'Superman is not looked at as a tragic figure at all, but vampires are because they're human first,' Rob explained to www.teenhollywood.com. 'In *Twilight*, Carlisle, who's the head of the Cullen clan, only turns people into vampires from his own guilt, when they're already about to die. They're virtually always unconscious when he does it, so they don't really have a choice. And then, they wake up. So, it's a good thing and a bad thing, at the same time. The only reason they really respect Carlisle is because he is kind of a saint. He's never killed anyone, but everyone else has, apart from Alice.'

So that was the Cullens as a whole, but what about the specific role he was about to play? Rob had a take on that, too. Perhaps what was most significant about the part was that Edward would not be anything like as powerful a character if he was simply a nice guy eschewing human blood and saving people: there *had* to be a very dark edge to him that he must strive to overcome. Every romantic hero is flawed – even Mr Darcy is proud and arrogant – and in Edward's case, the flaw is a combination of bloodlust and despair. That *had* to be brought out, or the portrayal wouldn't work.

'Edward tries to be nice to people, but not really,' Rob continued to www.teenhollywood.com. 'That's what a lot of the story is about as well. Edward is deciding to go against his base instincts. He knows he's a vampire, and he knows that what vampires do is go around killing people. That's the whole point in being a vampire. In denying that, it's kind of boring. If you're a human, you can go around doing whatever you want, at all times. I think most people would choose to do that. And Edward, for some reason, decides he doesn't want to do that, and he's trying to figure out why he doesn't want to do that, the whole time. But I think the vampires who kill everyone make a lot more sense.'

Then there was the alluring side of the role. On one level, of course, Edward is a romantic hero because of his looks: someone so handsome could scarcely fail to attract women. But there had to be something else there, too. There had to be something within his character that made him desirable, because women, perhaps more than men, do tend to see beyond the surface layer of what they are looking at. Rob managed to find that depth, too.

'What I never really understood about his attractiveness, especially to young girls, is his gentlemanliness,' he told film.com. 'I thought that teenage girls like the dangerous aspect of males, and so I tried to emphasize the danger and make the more gentlemanly side of this character a veil to something else underneath. I really tried to make him an incredibly strong and powerful character, but at the same time self-loathing and extremely vulnerable.'

It was this combination of strength, danger and vulnerability that really gave Rob's interpretation of the role its power. He had got to the core of what made Edward attractive as a character, and he was absolutely right that Edward needed to have a threatening edge. He was, after all, a potential killer, and while that might have been a tragedy for him, in that he didn't want to be, it made him extraordinarily dangerous to everyone else. The kissing scenes, in particular, are moments not only of great elation for Bella, but terrible peril, as well. That is the crux of what makes the series so compelling: the double edge of desire and threat, and Rob was to bring that out masterfully.

At the forefront of both Rob and the film-makers' minds was the key scenario that although Edward and Bella are massively attracted to each other, they don't actually ever have sex (in this film, at least). Thwarted lust is, of course, massively sexier than its fulfilment. In addition, there is a chance here that all that passionate longing may go nowhere, which is another crucial element of the film. 'So many younger girls are obsessed with this character and all that desire. The success of the books does, I think, come from the fact that fans can yearn and lust after Edward, and yet certainly in the first book, there's no actual sexual contact,' Rob explained to the *Daily Telegraph*.

And so the great juggernaut that was the film of *Twilight* set off. It was to alter Rob's life completely. Near the beginning of the making of the film, he was asked if he wanted to be famous: 'I can't see any advantage to it, because I'm happy with the life I have now,' he told *ES* magazine. 'I've got the same two friends I've had since I was twelve, and I can't see that changing.'

He was wrong. His life was about to change more than he, or anyone else, could possibly expect.

nine *twilight* tuesday

Rob had seen it all before, of course. When he had been Cedric Diggory – in that other phenomenally popular film involving schoolkids and the supernatural – he had witnessed a level of interest-cum-hysteria that had broken box-office records on a worldwide scale. In fact, such was the hoopla surrounding *Harry Potter*, he had chosen to go off and sit in the shadows for a couple of years, before, courtesy of *Twilight*, venturing out once again.

Yet it was somewhat different. In the *Harry Potter* pandemonium, Rob was not the main event. That honour had gone to the central trio of Daniel, Rupert and Emma – and even then, even Daniel was not quite the object of longing that Rob was going to become. Harry Potter was not an object of fantasy: however much J. K. Rowling might have tried to sex him up in the later books, he was essentially an Everyman, remembered as the little boy who lives in a cupboard under the stairs until he is rescued and taken to a land of magic.

Edward wasn't anything remotely like that. His purpose in the books right from the word go was to serve as the love object, the romantic hero. He and Bella gave each other's lives meaning. He was the ultimate fantasy figure – and Rob, being the actor who played him, was fast becoming that too.

Nothing in the world could have prepared Rob for the level of interest that was shown in him now. Having recanted so very publicly from their earlier doubts, Rob's admirers almost seemed to be wanting to make it up to him, practically foaming at the mouth whenever a picture of their hero appeared, let alone the man himself.

An unprecedented amount of attention was being paid to a film that was not only not yet out on general release, but hadn't even finished filming, with innumerable websites set up to chart the progress of the film and the man. A group existed called 'Twilight Moms': it had 4,000 members. MTV News created 'Twilight Tuesday', named after the day on which they would bring updates to the fans. Countless other teen and film websites regularly treated their readers to pictures, snippets of gossip and, more often than not, interviews with members of the cast. For Rob, Kristen, Taylor and the rest of them were all expected to do their bit. The film was clearly going to be a sensation, but the producers weren't taking any chances. Everyone was expected to contribute to the publicity effort – and how.

Not that the cast was aware of that frenzy from the very beginning. Holed up in Oregon where the shoot was taking place, far away from the action, they were simply concentrating on getting things done. The first scene they shot was actually one of the last scenes in the book: the huge fight in the dance studio, in which James the tracker vampire nearly manages to kill Bella, before the Cullens arrive in the nick of time.

It was quite a scene to kick off with, for on top of its patent dramatic and character demands, it involved a huge amount of other issues which required concentration – for example, the wire work. This is one of the techniques used for special effects in films and it means, quite literally, that the actors are wired up in order to take part in stunts. That is how the running sequences were filmed: Rob was wired up in order that he could actually run much faster than usual, and then more special effects were added in the editing room.

So, it was only when the cast returned to Los Angeles towards the end of the full filming session in Oregon, to do some more work in LA, that they began to realize that what they had created was turning into a sensation. Two hundred people turned up to meet them upon their arrival, and although that was nothing to the crowds that were to follow, this was, of course, before filming had even come to an end.

Back on the set itself, it was obvious that a bond was forming between Rob and Kristen. One visitor to the filming noted that, in between takes, she would go off and sit by herself to get into character; when it was time to return, it was Rob who would go over, give her a shoulder rub and bring her back. To help his interpretation of Edward, he himself, meanwhile, had been given access to something that only three other people in the world had seen at that point, and one of them was its author. It was the manuscript of *Midnight Sun*, which retold the *Twilight* story from Edward's point of view.

'Apart from [Stephenie] and the editor, just me and Catherine [Hardwicke have read it],' he told MTV News on one of its visits to the set for '*Twilight* Tuesday'. 'It is very top secret. And it is like halfway, two-thirds finished. I read that right at the beginning [of filming]. I got a lot of stuff out of that. It's exactly the same events, but a couple of other things happen. You get the same gist, but it's funny how different things affect Edward in ways that you don't really expect if you have just read *Twilight*.'

Indeed, with the first book told solely from Bella's perspective – and with her not being the mind-reader Edward himself was – there was a lot of 'blank canvas' surrounding his character, something that had really appealed to Rob. 'That is what I liked about [taking on] the job,' he said, 'because the guy doesn't really exist that much, so you can just create whatever you want.'

Of course, with Stephenie thoughtfully allowing Rob to read *Midnight Sun*, some of those blanks, which Rob had been imagining for himself, were now filled in by the creator of the *Twilight* universe. And the text made for a very encouraging read. 'When I found out there was another book from Edward's perspective, [I read it and it turned out] we had the same perspective!' declared Rob, excitedly.

The Edward of *Midnight Sun* is certainly a tortured soul. This is the love story told from the point of view of the vampire himself, rather than the human, and it reveals a being lost in misery at what he has become, before he finally finds some form of redemption through his relationship with Bella. Not that Edward realizes it at first. So violent is his attraction towards Bella that her life is in far more danger than is apparent in *Twilight*: early on, Edward is on the verge of killing her, thus revealing himself to be a vampire and turning his back on all the humanity Carlisle has taught him.

As we know, this had always very much been Rob's interpretation of the role. He had always rather enjoyed the idea of Edward's dark side: the fact that if he was a vampire, he must have a past and that past might well contain some unpalatable elements. As usual for Rob, he was far more interested in Edward as a complicated creature than Edward as a heart-throb, and here was the validation he needed that he had got his interpretation of the role spot on.

As an aside on *Midnight Sun*, it famously did not stay top secret for long. In August 2008, twelve chapters of the manuscript were illegally leaked on the Internet, without the permission or knowledge of Stephenie or her publisher. Sadly, following this upsetting experience, Stephenie felt she could not continue to write the book, which was at that time unfinished, and to this day the project remains on hold. Stephenie eventually took the decision to publish the leaked chapters on her website, saying, 'This way, my readers don't have to feel they have to make a sacrifice to stay honest.' Fans are hoping she will return to the novel, but at the time of writing there is no update to report.

Meanwhile, back on the set of *Twilight*, Kristen was emphasizing the need to take the film totally seriously, not just in terms of the huge amounts of money everyone was expected to make out of it, but in terms of the integrity of the story. The magnificence of the film sometimes threatened to overwhelm the love story at the centre of it, and she was very keen to ensure that the actors never lost sight of the essence of the story, as well as all the thrills that were being filmed along the way.

'In the big action sequences, it's a little scary because some people say, "We're going to get done with the action sequences, and then we'll get to the acting scenes,"' she told MTV. 'And it's like, "Well, that's just not how it works, man." It's hard to keep what you're doing in the rest of the movie consistent. You can't lose what's going on with the characters. [Action scenes] are actually more difficult, because you have to strive to not let it go and not just focus on a wall that's being ripped out or something. In the more intimate scenes, you're given the time to get into it.'

By the time of the Comic-Con convention in San Diego, alluded to in the first chapter, *Twilight* mania was in full swing. Quite apart from anything else, it was a relief for everyone behind the film to see the incredible reception the cast received, for an awful lot was riding on this: in the very unlikely event that *Twilight* was a flop, both money and reputations would be down the pan. That didn't look very likely though, as Stephenie pointed out. 'All of these screaming people want to see the right movie,' Stephenie told reporters present. 'We've got the right company, the right script and the right cast.'

Indeed, it all appeared to be going so brilliantly that the cast was beginning to talk about a second film, although nothing was to be finally confirmed until Summit assessed the market for the first one. 'I set my performance up to make it satisfying to do at least two more,' confessed Rob to E! Online. 'I don't know if they're going to make them or not, but I think they probably will.'

Taylor was a little more cautious. 'Nothing's been confirmed yet,' he said. 'So we're waiting to see. If it goes well, then maybe.'

But it certainly seemed to be going well. By now, Summit was beginning to release teasers, the odd scene here and there. MTV was no longer just running news stories and interviews: it was showing clips of the film, as well. *CosmoGirl* ran an extended feature on Rob, Taylor and Kellan (who plays Emmett), and their characters: Edward is 'a poet and very deep and profound', said Rob to the magazine. 'He's just extraordinarily troubled.' He was also 'conflicted and reluctant'. These hints revealed that this was clearly going to be a very edgy performance on the screen.

In July, the publicity machine cranked up yet another notch when *Entertainment Weekly* put Rob and Kristen on the cover, as the characters of Edward and Bella. They looked magnificent: Rob's shirt was open to reveal a toned, albeit pale, physique; the hair had been tamed somewhat, although there was still a great deal of it flopping about; his mouth was blood red. Vampiric elements aside, his appearance was redolent of the dancer Rudolf Nureyev as a young man, and while Rob played down all that work with the personal trainer, his physique really did look impressively fit and taut. In his arms was lucky Kristen, her long hair billowing out behind her, in a pale chiffon gown. In her hand she held a red apple: the fruit of temptation. Were the two of them going to bite into forbidden fruit?

Inside, there were more pictures of the cast, and ruminations by Catherine Hardwicke on the casting for the film. Kristen as Bella was a shoe-in: 'Her mixture of innocence and longing just knocked me out,' said Catherine, recalling the audition. 'She'd been shooting all night, but she learned her lines on the spot. She danced on the bed and chased pigeons in the park. I was captivated.'

As for Rob – 'Everybody has such an idealized vision of Edward,' said Catherine, with commendable understatement. 'They were rabid [about who would be cast]. Like old ladies saying, "You better get it right."'

Of course, given the fuss when Rob was picked, quite a few felt she hadn't done so, although by this stage no one was in much doubt that he was anything other than an inspired choice. Indeed, interest in the feature and the stars was so great that *EW* actually increased its print run for that edition.

One interesting feature of the pictures in the magazine is that Rob/Edward looks far more stylized than he does in the film. These were absolutely not the vampires of the old school, with fangs and talons, and yet there was the need for the magazine to make them look otherworldy. This was partly achieved by making everyone incredibly pale, but in Rob's case, as they'd singled him out as the focus of the shoot, this actually meant he looked like a very pale person rather than completely otherworldy.

In the film's promotional pictures and on the poster, which had first been released back in May, he looks far more like a supernatural being: skin even paler than it is in the movie, eyes glowing golden, and the mouth very red. The poster showed Edward, with burning amber eyes, standing protectively against the figure of Bella. Those famous glowing eyes were achieved by using contact lenses, one of the few downsides Rob encountered when making the film. They were painful and, he thought (erroneously), hampered his acting ability.

'Wearing coloured contact lenses ... It was like I constantly had sand in my eyes,' he told *OK!* magazine. 'I was wearing them for three months constantly and my eyes never, ever accepted them. It took me twenty minutes per eye every single day and I ended up having to literally fold it into my eyeball. It was frustrating as well because normally your eyes are saying something, but if you've got two orange blobs in your face it's so annoying. The director would say, "Look at her [Kristen] like you love her," and I'd be like, "I'm trying!"' In the end, of course, it was perfectly all right.

Edward's eyes are, in fact, quite a feature of the book. When his need for blood (animal, of course) has been sated, they glow a golden amber. But when the bloodlust rises up within him, then his eyes turn darker and darker, until they are nearly black. It's one of Bella's first clues that her boyfriend-to-be is a little unusual – although fortunately none of the other kids in the school ever catch on.

That same month, July 2008 – which was turning into quite a time for *Twilight* and everyone involved – both Rob and Kristen made it onto the list of Top-Twenty Rising Stars Under Thirty, chosen by *Saturday Night Magazine* (*SNM*). Kristen ranked at number two, while Rob came in sixth. A comparison that had first been made three years previously now came up again. Talking about Rob's 'buzz factor', *SNM* wrote that, 'Based on the hype surrounding *Twilight*, we're betting that by the time the film releases ... and starts raking in serious box-office cash, Pattinson should be well on his way to becoming the next Jude Law.'

Actually, by this point it was becoming increasingly obvious that Rob was going to far outdo anything ever managed by Jude Law: even at the height of his popularity, Law had never provoked anything like the hysteria that now followed Rob everywhere he went. Rob was stepping into a different league, and *SNM*'s endorsement of him was proof of it: there was no question but that he was well on track for a glorious career.

And there was soon a further sign that *Twilight*'s three central actors – Rob, Kristen and Taylor – were moving into the superstar stratosphere. It was revealed that they would be appearing at that autumn's MTV Video Music Awards: a prime-time slot that only the really, truly famous could aspire to. It seemed that nothing could stand in the way of the phenomenon's world domination.

Speaking of which, as summer wore on, there was an interesting announcement. The latest *Harry Potter* film, *Harry Potter and the Half-Blood Prince*, had been due to make its debut in the cinemas in November, a few weeks ahead of *Twilight*: it was suddenly announced that the film would premiere in the summer of 2009 instead, while *Twilight* would be released early, on 21 November 2008. There was heated speculation that the *Potter* rescheduling was because the makers of the movie were worried about a potential clash with *Twilight* – though everyone involved in both films was adamant that that had not been the case.

Even so, there was enough bad feeling that Stephenie Meyer felt compelled to write about it on her blog: 'So, many of you have heard that the release of the sixth *Harry Potter* movie, *Harry Potter and the Half-Blood Prince*, has been moved from this Thanksgiving to next summer,' she said. 'First and foremost, please know that this schedule change has absolutely nothing to do with *Twilight*, me, or Summit Films (so enough with the imdb [Internet Movie Database] death wishes, okay?). This is Warner Bros.'s decision, and it was not motivated by anything *Twilight*-related.' The tone was light, but the implication was clear: *Harry Potter* fans were boiling mad.

Come October, there was another groundswell of excitement when the theme song for *Twilight* was announced, which was to be recorded by Paramore. Paramore are a band from Tennessee, formed in 2004; they have since become firm teen favourites. The lead singer is Hayley Williams, who also plays keyboards, with the remaining members of the outfit comprising Josh Farro on guitar, Jeremy Davis on bass guitar and Zac Farro on drums. Hayley is herself a *Twilight* fan, and as pleased as anyone else about getting caught up in the film.

'*Twilight* is the first series of books I've ever read,' she told MTV. 'I didn't get into the *Harry Potter* series, even though I love the movies. *Twilight* really caught my attention and held it. I'm really excited to see the book adapted to film and excited that our band gets to be a part of the phenomenon.'

Hayley went on to explain that 'Decode', the theme song, had been wholly inspired by the Bella–Edward story. 'I chose the title "Decode" because the song is about the building tension, awkwardness, anger and confusion between Bella and Edward. Bella's is the only mind Edward can't read and I feel like that's a big part of the first book and one of the obstacles for them to overcome. It's one added tension that makes the story even better.'

The video for the song was to come out about three weeks before the premiere of the film, and would feature both the landscape of and clips from the movie. It was literally music to fans' ears – and all part of the gigantic publicity machine chugging ever faster into action.

In the wake of the Paramore announcement, and about six weeks before *Twilight* was due to premiere, Summit finally released the full track listing for the film. It's no secret that music was incredibly important to the creation of the *Twilight* series, and so it was no surprise that both the studio and the fans were taking a keen interest in this aspect of the film.

For a start, Stephenie Meyer considered music to have had such a significant role in the writing of the books that in her acknowledgements she frequently thanked the musicians who had inspired her, including Linkin Park, Travis, Coldplay, My Chemical Romance and many more. Her greatest praise was always reserved for the aptly-named Muse, to whom she eventually dedicated *Breaking Dawn*. 'There are emotions, scenes and plot threads in this novel that were born from Muse songs and would not exist without their genius,' she wrote, as an example of her tributes, at the start of *New Moon*.

She went further still on her website: 'I can't write without music. This, combined with the fact that writing *Twilight* was a very visual, movie-like experience, prompted me to collect my favourite *Twilight* songs into a sort of [personal] soundtrack for the book. This list is not chiselled in granite; it transforms now and again. But, for the moment, here's the music I hear in my head while reading the book' – and there followed a playlist of songs.

So, perhaps more than with any other film in recent memory, the movie's soundtrack was intricately linked to the plot, the characters and the overall atmosphere. Fans were well aware of Stephenie's love of and respect for music, and expected the film's creators to give plenty of attention to the OST. Consequently, a great deal of consideration was given to the musicians who made the final cut. In this order, the track listing read:

Muse – 'Supermassive Black Hole'
Paramore – 'Decode'
The Black Ghosts – 'Full Moon'
Linkin Park – 'Leave Out All the Rest'
MuteMath – 'Spotlight' (*Twilight* Mix)
Perry Farrell – 'Go All the Way (Into the Twilight)'
Collective Soul – 'Tremble for My Beloved'
Paramore – 'I Caught Myself'
Blue Foundation – 'Eyes on Fire'
Rob Pattinson – 'Never Think'
Iron & Wine – 'Flightless Bird, American Mouth'
Carter Burwell – 'Bella's Lullaby'

There was one very familiar name on that list. In fact, two of Rob's compositions were going to appear in the film, which made him rather unusual compared to most actors. While 'Never Think' was on the soundtrack, 'Let Me Sign' played in the movie itself, at the end of the climactic scene in the ballet studio. 'His two songs are pretty great,' director Catherine Hardwicke said.

It was another musician, however, who had crafted the most important song from the film: Bella's lullaby. This is a small but crucial part of the book. Edward (like Rob himself) is a musician

– a pianist – and composes the piece for his great love, partly as an outlet for and demonstration of his constant thoughts about her. The song assumes a greater importance still in the second novel, when Edward first makes a CD of his composition as a gift, and then hides it from Bella in an attempt to deny its existence, as he tries to convince himself they must stay apart.

In the film of *Twilight* – which of course had an aural element not available to the book – the lullaby provided a unique opportunity to express the nature of the central relationship and transfix the audience with a beautiful melody. With Rob seeming to have captured the character of Edward so brilliantly, there had been intensive speculation that he would put another of his talents, that of songwriting, to good use and compose the lullaby himself. In the event, however, the composer Carter Burwell, a veteran of the film industry who had created the film's score, was asked to write the song. This ensured a seamless transition between the lullaby and the underscore, and made sense on a thematic level too.

Yet it emerged that Rob had actually composed an original version of the lullaby, though this would never be released. He'd played it on set when they first shot the piano-playing scene, as the Burwell tune was not then available. As usual, he was characteristically philosophical about his being cut.

'We reshot the "Bella's lullaby" scene with a different piece of music,' he explained to MTV. 'I heard my original one the other day, and I really liked it. I was kind of depressed afterwards, but I like the new one as well. The new one I didn't write; the composer Carter Burwell did it. The new one fits in with the rest of the score, whereas my one was completely random, so unless you want a five-minute scene of just me playing the piano, I guess it's kind of irrelevant.'

Although Rob's lullaby didn't make the cut, it was still tremendously exciting that his other compositions had. For in truth, this was the first time that Rob had ever recorded music that was guaranteed to be released to the public, even though he had been a keen musician for years – of which more anon.

On 10 November, the '*Twilight* Talent Tour' began. This involved members of the cast making personal appearances to talk about the film, both in the United States and in selected cities in various parts of the world. Although Rob had been making personal appearances for some months now, it was nevertheless nerve-racking work – made all the more so by the fact that the cast didn't do one tour all together. Edi Gathegi (who played Laurent), Rachelle and Taylor were sent out as a trio, but Rob and Kristen both had to do their tours alone.

Rob had been the subject of an increasing amount of attention ever since it was announced that he had got the role of Edward, but now that began to step up a gear – or five. He began to discover that his life had changed beyond repair. Just nine months previously, he had been able to move about in relative anonymity: now he couldn't go outside with being mobbed. That had been most forcibly brought home back at the Comic-Con convention, when thousands of girls had screamed their heads off just because they were in close proximity to their hero, but these days a simple trip to the shops was becoming an ordeal.

It could be frightening. Rob was beginning to long to get back to what was familiar. The great irony was that he didn't really want this kind of attention. Genuinely shy and sometimes introverted, he was almost becoming a heart-throb in spite of himself. Many actors spend their lives attempting to get the kind of spotlight now trained on Rob: the man who had actually got it, however, didn't seem to want to be there. There was so much to concentrate on in the making and promoting of the film that Rob didn't have too much time to sit and brood about the fact that millions of people now thought he was possibly the most attractive man in the world – but the nuttiness of it all, the intensity, was definitely getting to him at times.

'I was getting quite scared the other day,' he told FEARnet, when he was visiting Philadelphia as part of the tour. 'When I go back to London, the only thing I've done all year [will be to have gone] around to cities and have people scream at me and stuff, and ask things like, "What's it like to play the most beautiful person in the world?" I'm going to go back and start talking to my friends, being like, "Yeah, well, this other person asked me how is it to play the most beautiful person in the world and then I went to this room and there's five thousand people screaming at me." I feel like I have nothing to talk about to my friends anymore. It's going to really destroy me when I go back home.'

He was beginning to face the dilemma suffered by everyone who starts to experience extreme fame, as opposed to being merely very well known. Rob's friends were of crucial importance to him and kept him grounded, but they couldn't have any idea what he was going through at the moment. Only the other cast members, especially Kristen, could have had a clue as to what his life was now like. His growing stature was making people change the way they talked to him: like it or not, except amongst the Hollywood elite, Rob was no longer 'one of us'. He was starting to feel it, too.

'It's so new to me I can't really be jaded,' he told FEARnet. 'It's not really going to my head because I don't even know what it is. It's strange how you get treated differently by people in a very brief amount of time. When you ask someone to go out to dinner, they're like, "Do you want me to?" It's like, "What are you talking about, why would I have asked you?!" Funny little things like that happen.'

And they were happening more and more. But he certainly retained his sense of humour. When *Metromix Baltimore* asked him how much of a sexy man-beast he was, Rob replied, 'I wouldn't be able to say. I don't think I'm much of one. It's funny, it is the secret for any guy – if people find him unattractive or whatever – you just get Stephenie Meyer to tell the world, to put on her website that this guy is now attractive and everybody changes their minds.' He was still refusing to acknowledge his own attractiveness: this, of course, simply added to the allure.

The week before the film opened, *Entertainment Weekly* had Rob and Kristen back on its cover – Rob looking less vampiric and slightly more like a human being – and a selection of exclusive pictures inside. Showings for the opening weekend were selling out fast, and had been even several weeks in advance.

And so, 17 November 2008 – the date scheduled for the US premiere – finally dawned. The build-up to this event had been such that the cast and public alike had been living in a state of being almost permanently on edge. Now that D-day (or should that be T-day?) had at last arrived, it was actually something of a relief. At least once the film was out there, it could mark a return to some semblance of normality, for Rob and everyone else. (In Rob's case, of course, that was not actually going to happen, but at least his portrayal would be in the open and there would no longer be the endless worry about what everyone was going to think.)

The Mann Village Theater in LA, where the premiere took place (as described in the first chapter of this book), was well used to fan hysteria – but this was as nothing even that famous building had seen before. Later, a new name for the impact the film was having would be coined – fangdemonium. That was what greeted Rob and the cast as they stepped onto the red carpet that night; it was what greeted them at every other *Twilight* premiere around the world over the next few weeks.

Indeed, the response *was* universal. Pretty much across the board, from fans and critics alike, the film received a thumbs-up. Viewing the movie, that was far from a surprise. Rob's performance in the film was everything that could have been hoped for – and more. And that much-talked-about chemistry between him and Kristen couldn't be missed: when the two appeared together, there seemed to be an electrical current between them, binding them together like invisible glue.

Rob had, in fact, judged his performance perfectly. There was a hint of menace in the way he moved, even, at times, towards Kristen. He, and the other Cullens, were set apart from the others at the school, not just because of their striking appearance, but because of an aloofness that made it clear they belonged in another realm. The sheer beauty of the film, especially in the scene in which Rob/Edward is exposed to sunlight and his skin begins to glitter, had a poetic quality to it. Even the town of Forks looked lush.

This was a step forward for Rob in other ways, too. In the *Harry Potter* films, his portrayal of Cedric was as the slightly uptight English public schoolboy, a romantic rival to Harry, a fourteen-year-old boy. Now Rob – a man, no longer a boy – had come into his own. This was a man who was passionately in love, a teenager by virtue of his seventeen years, perhaps, but displaying a maturity and depth of emotion Rob had not shown on-screen before. It displayed a range to his talents that did down the naysayers. It suggested a lengthy career ahead.

The critics agreed. 'Serious and clenched, a Heathcliff for adolescents, he's also a bionic superhero who appears from nowhere to save her from the clutches of growly bad boys and has merely to stretch out an immaculately muscled arm to stop cars crashing into her,' wrote Sukhdev Sandhu of Rob in the *Daily Telegraph*, adding of the film in general, and its director: 'Hardwicke, though, understands that the novels tap into a yearning that a particular kind of adolescent cultivates for a deeper, richer form of romance that seems masochistic and depressing only to outsiders. I watched *Twilight* in a cinema full of young girls who, when they weren't texting friends and guzzling soft drinks, giggled, sighed and exhaled with a passion that was not only endearing, but a measure of its emotional truth.'

Chris Tookey in the *Daily Mail* was also a fan. 'The character he plays in *Twilight* – Edward Cullen, a high-school vampire trying to control his lust for teenage female flesh – is a Lord Byron for our times: if not mad and bad, certainly dangerous to know,' he wrote. 'The zeitgeist is so stacked in this film's favour that whatever I think of it has no relevance to whether it is a hit. It will be. But the reality is that it does hit the spot as a tale of forbidden love and virtually endless, smouldering foreplay: *Dirty Dancing* without the class issues, *High School Musical* without the sex.'

'It's hard not to read this as some slightly sinister metaphor for the perils of fornication and the wonders of abstinence, yet at the same time there is something tantalizingly swoony about impossibly elusive gratification' was Trevor Johnston's view in *Time Out*. 'With brooding mist-wreathed mountains an effective backdrop, the key performers strike sparks from the electric tension of not-quite-kissing.'

James Christopher, in *The Times*, was also impressed. '*Twilight* is a supernatural sex education movie for lovesick goths. It's a terrifically potty fantasy about a pale and moody teenage girl, Bella (Kristen Stewart), who falls in love with an even paler and moodier boy in her gloomy new high school in the middle of rainswept nowhere,' he wrote. 'The anguish is exquisite ... Edward vents his frustration on local jocks who foolishly try to jump his girlfriend in dark alleys. The supernatural stunts don't disappoint. Neither does the deadpan wit.'

Reviews in the United States were a little less complimentary, with the consensus that it could be a little schmaltzy, but who cared? The film was turning into the hit everyone had been predicting, and Rob's performance was generally felt to have carried a perfect Edward to the screen. Sometimes playful, sometimes brooding, he did manage the very difficult task of conveying his dual role: a teenager in love, who is at the same time an ancient creature driven by bloodlust. The American accent was impeccable (in an interview, when asked if it was more difficult to portray someone who was American or who was supernatural, he went for the latter), and the intensity of feeling he illustrated was entirely in keeping with the tone of the book.

One or two reviews said that the chemistry between Rob and Kristen was not what it should be, but that was just plain silly: the two of them fizzed off each other. Rob spoke repeatedly about how much he admired his co-star, and how much her interpretation of the role drew him in – so much so, in fact, that there were rumours that his feelings towards her were more than just professional.

The only trouble with that was that Kristen already had a boyfriend, Michael Angarano. Like Kristen, Michael was a child actor. Born on 3 December 1987 in New York, Michael first appeared on-screen in *Almost Famous* when he was thirteen; his major breakthrough came in 2002 in *Little Secrets*. Two years after that, he appeared in the film *Speak*: his co-star was Kristen, and the two became an item shortly afterwards. It was a relationship that was to last for five years, and was still going strong during the *Twilight* era. Consequently, both Kristen and Rob denied being involved with one another, although typically that wasn't enough to dampen the hot gossip. Naturally, it wasn't exactly going to hurt the film if it was rumoured that its two major stars were involved off-screen as well as on.

The only other bone of contention where the film was concerned was more a sign of the lax moral times we live in than anything else: because it is dangerous even for Bella and Edward to kiss, let alone do anything else, the film was seen in some quarters as propaganda for Stephenie's religious views. Perhaps it was, but in not understanding the strength of feeling that thwarted passion can produce in the viewer, those critics rather missed the point.

Regardless of the reviews, though, both good and bad, the craziness was running out of control. The cast was touring the world with the film now, living out of hotels and suitcases, as it premiered in different time zones and languages: Rob was a long way from home. And at times it seemed as if it overwhelmed him. 'I've been going to different cities all around the world in the past three weeks to these planned events where everybody just screams and screams and screams,' he told the *Daily Mirror*, sounding more like the little boy his sisters used to dress up and call Claudia than the confident young film star he had essentially become. 'Every single time I get so nervous and have cold sweats – I doubt that I am ready [for stardom]. I started crying in Italy, completely involuntarily.'

But what could he do? This was Rob's life now – and, in his heart, he wouldn't have wanted to change it if he could. For all the nerve-racking quality of the attention he was currently receiving, opportunities were opening up that he couldn't have dreamt of before. And anyway, the hype would die down in time, surely.

Or would it? Was Rob's star to shine even brighter than before?

ten who's dating whom?

As the most momentous year in Rob's life, 2008, began to draw to an end, interest in Rob only began to hot up even further. *Twilight* the movie had been everything that fans of the book had hoped for and plans for the second film, *New Moon*, were now underway.

Rob himself was under intensive scrutiny, not least as far as his love life was concerned: though he was adamant that he was single, rumours linking him to Kristen just refused to go away. Kristen herself, who was still enmeshed with Michael, was beginning to sound exasperated: 'I've made a very dear friend and that's worth more than anything,' she snapped. Rob, too, when questioned about the rumour, sounded a little weary. 'They're so ridiculous at the film company,' he said in an interview with *The Times*. 'They keep refusing to deny it. They just say, "No comment." And we're like, "We're not."'

And, in truth, his 'relationship' with Kristen was by no means the only rumour circulating. Rob was being linked to plenty of other women, including the Brazilian model Annelyse 'Anne' Schoenberger, his co-star Nikki Reed, Erika Dutra, Paris Hilton, Natalie Portman, Megan Fox, Camilla Belle, Shannon Woodward and just about anybody else he met along the way. There was constant questioning about whether he'd ever been in love – Rob was vague – and at one point he appeared to give up on relationships altogether. 'I don't see people,' he told *GQ* magazine in March 2009. 'I don't even have people's phone numbers. I almost don't want to have a girlfriend in this environment.' Groupies could have been a possibility, were Rob that way inclined, given the number of women throwing themselves at him, but Rob appeared shocked to the core by the very thought.

Rob's aunt Monica Weller gave some insight into this. Back in Britain, the family had been watching with a combination of pride and concern about Rob's growing stardom, and they, too, would have known what excitements would be offered along the way. This was, however, a danger. While no one expected Rob to live like a monk, young men presented with such opportunities, so suddenly, had been known to destroy themselves. But Monica felt there was no danger of that.

'I could say there were signs when he was growing up he was going to be a heartbreaker,' she told the *National Enquirer*. 'He was always a good-looking boy and he does have a special something that makes people want to watch him. But at the same time, he is really just a very normal boy, with manners and charm, and I think girls find those qualities attractive. [Our family] was brought up not to give in to temptations like that. He gets his strength of character from the family, it's in his genes.'

Of course, no one could believe that this spectacularly handsome young man was really single: surely there were women queuing up to be seen on his arm? Rob addressed the subject in an interview with the *Mirror*, in which he said that his new profile was actually making it difficult to think about a relationship. 'I'm not dating anyone at the moment,' he said. 'But it's weird. If you try and chat people up, it's like, "Oh, you're just an actor. You probably go around sleeping with everybody." So fame has the opposite effect of what you'd expect.'

The rumour that really did refuse to go away, however, was that Rob was sweet on Kristen, and was hoping their relationship was going to grow into something more. Everyone, including Rob, Kristen and Catherine Hardwicke, had commented on the chemistry between the two of them, and it is not unusual for on-screen chemistry to exist off-screen as well.

And they had forged a bond through the making of the film. Kristen was already well known before she signed up for *Twilight*, while Rob had already experienced fan hysteria with *Harry Potter*, but this film was something else. The intensity of the interest in it – and, even more so, the people who were making it – was something that neither had encountered before. In many ways, only Rob and Kristen could know what the other was going through. Relationships have been founded on considerably less.

Rob certainly took every opportunity he had to praise her. 'Kristen's great,' he told *Random Interview*. 'She's one of the main reasons why I wanted to do this: just because of her body of work and also just the audition kind of made me feel very differently about it. I had no idea how to do it before the audition. I mean, she's an extraordinarily talented actress.' She also had a very strong personality – and Rob had said in the past that was one of the facets he found attractive in a woman.

Nor was there any indication that interest in the two of them was going to subside. As soon as the success of *Twilight* had been taken on board, plans for *New Moon* were put into play. There was some disappointment that Catherine Hardwicke would not be directing it. It seemed to be the case that she wanted more time to prepare, whereas Summit wanted to get cracking on the movie right away. Everyone, however, was keen to emphasize that they were all still good friends.

'Catherine did an incredible job in helping us to launch the *Twilight* franchise and we thank her for all of her efforts and we very much hope to work with her on future Summit projects,' said Erik Feig, Summit's President of Production, in one of his ongoing pronouncements about events surrounding the film. 'We as a studio have a mandate to bring the next instalment in the franchise to the big screen in a timely fashion so that fans can get more of Edward, Bella and all of the characters that Stephenie Meyer has created. We are able to pursue an aggressive time frame as we have the luxury of only adapting the novels into screenplays, as opposed to having to create a storyline from scratch.' In other words – they wanted to get on.

And well they might. *Twilight* went straight to number one at the box office in America, taking in $70 million, the highest debut ever for a female director, and has since grossed over $340 million worldwide. It also made the record books by being responsible for the third highest number of pre-release cinema-seat bookings in the US, behind only *The Dark Knight* and *Star Wars Episode III: Revenge of the Sith*. There were good reasons Summit wanted to strike while the iron – like the film's star – was so very hot.

For also significant in the scheduling decisions – as with *Harry Potter* – was the matter of the characters' ages. At twenty-two, Rob could just about get away with playing a seventeen-year-old, but his appearance was bound to change as he grew older, along with that of the rest of the cast. This was all very well as far as Bella and the rest of the humans were concerned, but the vampires were supposed to be stuck forever at the age they were when they

became vampires. Clearly, Summit needed to get their performances in the bag before the vampire characters started to look
like considerably older versions of themselves.

In the meantime, Rob began to start totting up all kinds of
acclaim for his work in the movie. Around the time the film was
released, *Entertainment Weekly* published its list of Ten Breakout
Stars for 2008: Rob topped the list, followed by Demi Lovato,
Russell Brand, Estelle, Shailene Woodley, David Cook, Tristan
Wilds, Kat Dennings, Chelsea Handler and Angel. This was a
high-profile and prestigious slot to take, and would certainly not
have damaged his standing in Hollywood – although that even
more important gauge, box-office success, was assuring him of a
great future there, too.

Again in the States, *TV Guide* named him as the Male Breakout
Star of 2008 (Kat Dennings was his female counterpart). In the UK,
Hello! magazine did the same: in this case, it was on the back of a
readers' poll, and Rob got two-thirds of the votes. AccessHollywood.
com named him as number ten on their list of most-searched-for
celebrities, and he was number fifteen in MuchMusic.com's 'Hottest
Stars of 2008' chart. He was honoured with the New Hollywood
Award at the Hollywood Film Festival. *Trendhunter* magazine
called him the 'Man of the Moment'. The *Huffington Post* put him on
its Best Trends of 2008 list, while Standard.net had him in the
Top-Five Best Actors of 2008. *USA Today* hailed him as one of 2008's
Hottest Breakthroughs – alongside Barack Obama. He could do
nothing wrong.

Rob, however, refused to get carried away by it all, maintaining
that he was the same person he ever was. It was the book and the
character of Edward that people were responding to, he maintained,
not Rob himself. 'So many young people who get a big hit kind of

get hyped up,' he told the *Philly Daily News*. 'They start to believe their own hype, and then everyone starts to, like, cut them down immediately. And I just feel like I'm being propelled by something I have absolutely no control over.'

This wasn't just modesty: it was survival. Constantly, Rob talked about his fear of crowds and how much he hated being mobbed. The personal appearances were an ordeal; he also confessed that it was sometimes tempting to stand up and say something pretty awful – but of course, that would be to self-destruct. And wearing as it might sometimes feel to be the focus of such attention, Rob was well aware that he had been offered the opportunity of a lifetime. Come through the uproar unscathed and he would, he knew, have an acting career set up for life.

He was going to be financially set up, too. It was not revealed how much Rob was getting paid for the role of Edward, but it's safe to assume it was well into seven figures, although he strenuously denied reports that it was $12 million (£8 million): 'If I [was] getting paid $12 million a movie, I'd walk around naked.' But he was gaining financial independence very early on in life, which would in turn give him leeway to work on smaller projects again, should he wish to do so. Importantly, he was not running wild and splashing his cash all over the shop: the frugality that had been obvious in his earlier life, when he'd adopted a very modest adolescent lifestyle, despite his lucrative modelling income, was still there.

Given that he was now such a hot property, he was massively in demand – but he was also in the very fortunate position of being able to pick and choose his parts. In the wake of *Twilight*, he had of course signed up for *New Moon*, but at that stage the only other film he'd considered was *Parts Per Billion*, alongside Dennis

Hopper, and a filming clash with *New Moon* meant he subsequently had to withdraw from that.

In all, the world was his oyster – but there were downsides. There remained signs that Rob was not coping well with all the attention. He continued to wrestle with some aspects of his sudden fame: 'I don't like going outside anymore,' he told TheImproper.com. 'It's so embarrassing to see pictures of yourself at the airport when you look terrible.' Naturally, Rob's fans didn't believe that he could look terrible, but Rob's innate self-deprecation led him to believe he simply couldn't be the looker everyone told him he was.

In truth, though, the most difficult aspect of being the world's hottest celebrity was not the (supposedly dodgy) paparazzi pictures that were being taken of him on a daily basis. Rob had never been keen on crowds in the first place – and now he couldn't get away from them, for the simple reason that they formed wherever he went.

'People ambush me in public and ask me to bite them and want to touch my hair,' he said to the *Daily Star*, sounding, in all honesty, a little hysterical. 'I just don't want someone to have a needle and give me AIDS and I don't want to get shot or stabbed. This is my life.' The LA premiere had shaken him, too: 'I thought, "Oh my God. Are they going to blow the place up?"' It was perhaps this that prompted a rather severe haircut just before Christmas – an all but crew cut. Given how famous Rob's hair had become, it made headlines all around the world.

His co-stars were aware of the pressure he was under. They were the subject of constant observation, too, but not quite to the same extent. Ashley Greene, who plays Alice, was sympathetic: 'Poor Rob is already a Beatle,' she said perceptively to *Nylon Guys* magazine. 'His whole life is documented. If he picks his nose, it's all over the Internet. He's just done for.'

But, of course, even the Beatles didn't have it quite as bad as this. There was no Internet in their heyday, and so information couldn't be flashed online the moment they did anything, which was not the case with Rob. Plus, there were four of them – so that they could not only provide moral support for one another, but also diffuse the fans' adulation so it was not focused solely on one man.

Yet despite the odd outburst, somehow Rob *was* coping with it all. His family was determined he should stay grounded, and he was; somehow, he was keeping his head. That modest sense of humour was crucial for this, along with the fact that Rob had not forgotten the initial negative reaction when it was announced that he was to take on the role of Edward. He knew he was in fashion; he also knew fashions change.

Nor was he entirely alone. Kristen also got her fair share of attention, and it made her as nervous as it did Rob. And that wasn't foolish, for there was a darker side to the fans' fixation on the actress who worked so closely with their hero. '[If you see] more than three girls a certain age [in a group] – run away,' she told a US newspaper. 'Girls are scary. Large groups of girls scare the crap out of me. They covet him [Rob]. I think half of them are so jealous they hate me.' She almost certainly had a point. For a start, many fans confused the actors in the film with their characters; and secondly, those rumours about her and Rob were still refusing to go away. Rob's name continued to be linked to other women, but none of the stories stuck and none of them turned into real relationships. The rumour mill churned on.

Behind all of this, the *Twilight* movie machine was cranking into action once more. Chris Weitz had by now been named as director of *New Moon*: his past credits included *American Pie*, *About a Boy* and *The Golden Compass*. There was some concern from fans that, as a man, Chris wouldn't be able to understand Bella's perspective, but Chris himself was adamant that this was not to be the case. In a letter to *Twilight* fans posted on Stephenie Meyer's website, he wrote, 'To those who doubt that as a male director I can capture Bella's experience, I can only say that emotion is universal and that my work has often involved working with some of the most talented actresses in the world. For the rest, the proof will have to be in the pudding.'

As work on the film began in earnest, the focus shifted somewhat from Rob to Taylor Lautner. Edward, after all, leaves Bella early on in the book, and doesn't return until quite near the end, when he believes she's died and decides to take his own life. A large and central part of the story is instead devoted to the growing friendship between Bella and Jacob, a relationship that grows so much he even becomes a potential romantic rival to Edward. Rob/ Edward was not required to carry the film in quite the same way that he had done before: it must have been a relief in many ways.

The story, however, was several degrees darker than its predecessor. Both Bella and Edward spend the novel and film in an advanced state of despair, and even when they are reunited, there are threats hanging over them, and the knowledge that they can only ever truly be together if Bella gives up her human state is harshly crystallized. Rob certainly saw the melancholic side of it all.

'The book of *New Moon*, the majority of it is incredibly depressing,' he told Reuters. 'Obviously *Twilight* was about finding first love and the difficulties of that, but *New Moon* is really about loss and reconciliation, but the reconciliation isn't completely full. It's a strange story to have for a market that, I guess, wants to see a love story.' But of course, it was, ultimately, a love story: merely one with a very unusual twist.

Early in 2009, *Little Ashes*, Rob's Dali film, got a release date, which was when Rob got into trouble for referring to it as a 'little film'. It was clear that he had not meant the comment to sound anything like as derogatory as it did, for he also gave a very thoughtful assessment of Dali's life and the role he played. He could even see a comparison between Dali and Edward Cullen. 'I think both of them were terrified,' he said in an interview in *The Independent*. 'Especially Dali. He had so many sexual hang-ups. He was crippled by so many different things.

'If you read some of his early-life autobiography, it's horrible ... the amount of mental anguish he has to go through, just to have any kind of even vaguely sexual relationship. It's really depressing what he's going through in his head. [...] To not betray or insult someone's memory, it seemed a lot more important than other jobs I've done before.'

Important jobs aside, Rob found that, come February 2009, he had some important dates in his diary: events that would really seal his status as a superstar. February, you see, is the awards season both in the UK and the US. Rob had not had much to do with it until now, but it was imperative that an actor of his growing stature join the circuit, and so first it was off to London, to attend the BAFTAs – where he was reacquainted with his fellow *Harry Potter* star Emma Watson – before flying back across the Atlantic for the big one. Rob was going to be attending the Oscars that year.

Indeed, Rob had been asked to present an award, a request he treated with total disbelief. 'It's insane,' he said to MTV News, as he lurked on the red carpet outside the Kodak Theatre in LA, before making his way inside. 'When they first told me about this, I was like, "No, no, no, no, no, you're joking – or I'm going to have to do something really stupid like get gunged!"'

In actual fact, that Oscars ceremony was yet another step along the road in his transition from teen star to global icon. The organizers of the 2009 event were determined to get Rob, now the hottest property on the planet, to attend, but in order to drum up anticipation, they refused to confirm who would or would not be a presenter until a couple of days before the ceremony. It was not a huge shock that Rob was one of the chosen ones, but it was a real endorsement of his increasing power and presence in Hollywood.

This was Rob's first time at the show and yet another sign of quite how far he had come: all around him were some of the most famous men and women in the world. The Oscars are always a fashion parade as much as anything else, and this year was no different: here Penelope Cruz (who won Best Supporting Actress for *Vicky Cristina Barcelona*) was stealing the show in white vintage Balmain; there Beyoncé was working her fishtail look in a black-and-gold flounced number by House of Dereon. Sarah Jessica Parker was in Dior haute couture; Anne Hathaway in Armani Prive; Heidi Klum in red Roland Mouret; and Natalie Portman wore a pink dress by Rodarte. Also out on the red carpet were Madonna, Jennifer Aniston, Meryl Streep, Nicole Kidman, Sophia Loren, Kate Winslet, the young Indian cast of *Slumdog Million-aire*, Brangelina … in short, some of the most glamorous and successful people on earth.

And yet a massive amount of the attention was focused on Rob, who was looking very dapper in a tuxedo, it has to be said. It was he who was most in demand as dozens of interviewers, accompanied by cameramen from television stations all around the world, waited their turn to speak with him. Characteristically, he dealt with the mind-blowing scenario in his usual, comic fashion: when Fearne Cotton asked him if he had a message for family and friends back home, the answer was, 'Hello, Mum.' To stand out in that company was an extraordinary achievement; a sign that Rob's fame was not just a fleeting *Twilight*-related phenomenon, but something that was set to last.

Of course, *Twilight* wasn't up for an award, but that wasn't the point. Neither was *High School Musical*, and yet Zac Efron was also there that night as a presenter: the organizers wanted hot, young glamour, and they got it. Even the host, Hugh Jackman, while slightly senior in years to the likes of Rob and Zac, was a representative of young Hollywood, rather than its more middle-aged counterpart. Rob was there to present a 'montage of love' from 2008, a role he performed with Amanda Seyfried, who had starred in *Mamma Mia*. No one had inspired more devotion than Rob over the previous year, and so no one was better qualified to perform that particular role.

The calibre of the other presenters selected alongside Rob and Zac neatly illustrated where the Brit now was in the Hollywood pecking order. Jennifer Aniston was one of the presenters; Alan Arkin, Jack Black, Robert De Niro, Michael Douglas, Whoopi Goldberg and various other Hollywood legends made up the rest of the roll call. Rob was now beginning to rub shoulders with these icons – as equals. Given that eighteen months previously, only a few die-hard fans actually knew who he was, that was some leap Rob had made.

He himself ended up finding the whole experience actually slightly *less* gruelling than previous public outings. 'It's much more organized than a *Twilight* premiere,' he said. 'At those, you feel like you are going to die.' All that screaming adoration was clearly still getting to him.

Of course, the Oscars ceremony is every bit as much about business as it is about glamour, and so are all the entertainments on offer afterwards. Meeting players and pressing the flesh is as crucial for making it in Hollywood as starring in big-name films, and so after the awards themselves, it was on to, first the Governor's Ball, and then the *Vanity Fair* party, held at the Sunset Tower Hotel in West Hollywood – one of the most prestigious locations in town. 'I'm really classy,' said Rob, as he turned down the champagne in favour of a beer, but more to the point, he was looking right at home.

That wasn't surprising, when you really thought about the situation and the nature of the lives of the company he was keeping. He was mixing with other massive stars, who also had to deal with adulation bordering on hysteria. Here, unlike anywhere else, people knew what it felt like to be Rob. One of these was Paris Hilton, herself the centre of a good deal of media attention: according to onlookers, she and her sister Nicky tracked Rob down in the confines of the party and 'flirted aggressively'. But the suspicion remained – his heart belonged to Kristen.

Indeed, Rob and Kristen shared the Best Kiss Award at the MTV Movie Awards, held in late May; an accolade they collected in person. Their appearance on stage threw the audience at Universal City's Gibson Amphitheatre into an absolute frenzy. The pair edged closer and closer together, as Rob's lips parted enticingly … until Kristen backed off. 'Thank you sooooo much,' she told the audience.

Were they hinting that their relationship really had gone

further? Were they deliberately muddying the waters in a (very successful) attempt to keep the world guessing? Was it a private tease? Neither Rob nor Kristen was telling – but hey: the fans were getting used to that by now.

As it turned out, the MTV Movie Awards proved to be quite a night for *Twilight* all round. The team won a total of five awards, including Best Film. Kristen was honoured with Best Actress, while Rob got Best Breakthrough Performance (Male). *Twilight* also won a prize for Best Fight, for the electrifying scene in the ballet studio. They were all delighted with their haul of accolades – and ever more keen to deliver the goods on the upcoming sequel.

Speaking of which, filming for *New Moon* started in late spring 2009: this time, it was mostly to take place in Vancouver, Canada. Rob was becoming used to living out of a suitcase, and now set up home in the unlikely surroundings of a windowless room high up on the thirtieth floor of a hotel. He was happy enough, talking about not even letting the maids in to change the sheets, because he didn't want them to see what was lurking in there. Naturally, the great advantage of a windowless room is that no one can see in, something Rob was clearly pleased about.

Somehow, the sense of humour remained. He couldn't bear to think about how famous he'd become, he told an interviewer from *The Guardian*, and disguises didn't work: 'Instead, I'm just getting more and more conspicuous; I'm wearing two hoods, a hat and sunglasses, which kind of stands out in the middle of the night. So I'm learning to sprint.'

Filming alongside him was the rest of the *New Moon* cast, which of course included some new additions, about which there had been great excitement. The British actor Jamie Campbell Bower had been cast as one of the Volturi leaders, Caius. Bizarrely, after completing the second *Twilight* film, Campbell Bower's next movie would be a *Harry Potter* one, for he had been chosen for the role of Gellert Grindelwald in *Harry Potter and the Deathly Hallows*. He and Rob therefore shared a unique bond amongst actors: the only two to have appeared in both franchises.

Other new members of the team included Michael Sheen, playing Aro, and Dakota Fanning, playing Jane (both members of the Volturi coven). Oscar-nominee Graham Greene also joined the cast, as Charlie's friend Harry Clearwater. With all the actors in place, fans could truly start imagining the vision of the sequel.

That May, Rob turned twenty-three – dangerously close to the upper age limit set for the actor who played Edward by Stephenie, although by now the role was so very much his own, it was inconceivable that anyone else could have been drafted in. A group from the film joined Rob in the Glowbal Grill and Satay Bar in Vancouver to celebrate: they included Kristen, Ashley Greene and Jamie Campbell Bower.

After champagne cocktails, according to *The People*, the party chowed down on kobe beef meatballs, lamb, steak, salads and roasted vegetables – a menu that became public because the group was being observed by hundreds of fans, who had gathered outside. Someone had posted Rob's location on Twitter and the news spread fast: Rob and his co-stars coped, however, and the man himself posed for pictures with some of his admirers before leaving for the restaurant's bar Afterglow. It was the price of fame, but he managed not to be too freaked out.

Rob was finding it a relief to be back on set, to a certain extent protected from the greater excesses of the fans, but he was still very much in the public eye. More superlatives began rolling in again. Readers of *Heat* magazine voted him the Sexiest Man Alive.

Vanity Fair named him Most Handsome Man in the World, after a readers' poll gave him 51 per cent of the votes: of the eighteen men on the list, number two was Nacho Figueras, with 15 per cent, and three was Brad Pitt, with 12 per cent. Rob didn't just win that competition: he stood out head and very broad shoulders above the rest. *People* also put him on its annual Best Bachelors list, declaring, 'Fangs are the new pecs.' In Britain, he was number three in *Company* magazine's Most Eligible Bachelors in Britain list, and the only surprise is that he didn't top that, too, beaten to the post by Prince Harry and presenter George Lamb.

As it had done with *Twilight*, MTV News was closely following *New Moon*. According to Rob, the pace of the second film was very different from the first. 'There's definitely a difference in scale,' he said. 'I liked doing *Twilight*, but it felt very like an indie movie – and [*New Moon*] definitely feels like it's a big movie.'

He was right there. It was more than a big movie: it was a fully formed franchise now, like the *Harry Potter* films, or the James Bond or Indiana Jones series. And while, at the time of writing, that franchise is confined to four novels, there is no saying that Stephenie Meyer might not change her mind and write another book about the Cullens. The film series had all the hallmarks of something that could run and run.

The new movie's poster was also launched in May: with Bella seemingly sheltered by Jacob, Edward glowers at them from the side – a symbol of the way in which Bella's loyalties are torn during the film. The launch was greeted with a frenzy of excitement, as Rob put in an appearance at the sixty-second Cannes Film Festival, where he attended a photo call at the waterfront, grinning at photographers and ruffling his hair. The pictures made worldwide headlines, as everything he touched seemed to, these days.

Photographers were not the only ones present on the beach at the Croisette: there was a crowd of screaming fans, too – kept at a distance, but getting as close to their hero as they were allowed to, nonetheless.

The sun beat down on the beach in the South of France as Rob talked to journalists about the making of the new film and how it was all going. He was feeling a lot more acceptance about the way he was such a focus of attention now, he said: after all, he'd had over a year of it by this stage, and he couldn't go on being surprised. The new film had been a pleasure to work on, he added, relaxing: all the more so as in the second part of the story he plays more of a supporting role.

How that narrative will go down with the fans is, of course, open to question – at the time of writing, the film has not yet been released. What was clear from the press conference was that Rob has finally accepted that, like it or not, he is the major heart-throb of his generation. It might not have been the role he thought he was born to play, but he was playing it awfully well.

While he was now coming to terms with his personal fame, though, he found that fans' reaction to the series as a whole never lost the power to amaze. 'It never ever fails to shock me,' Rob told *Metro*, talking from the film set. 'Even here. Yesterday, there were 300 people outside the set. It's just crazy. Every day, every single person I meet knows someone who has a very strong attachment to the books. It's very difficult to put your head around. I can go through customs at any airport in the world – every customs agent is like, "Can I get an autograph for my daughter?" Every single time! It's crazy! I just hope it doesn't change the way I think and stuff.' That seemed very unlikely, given his down-to-earth attitude.

The *New Moon* publicity machine was grinding away in earnest, now, with clips from the new movie posted on the Internet, and dropped snatches of information – fans learned that the cast was soon to move on to Italy to film the sequence in which Edward nearly brings about his own death at the hands of the Volturi.

Rob was certainly coming across as happier and more relaxed than he had done before. But perhaps the greatest irony of all is that the man who is undisputedly the world's favourite film star very nearly didn't go into acting at all.

eleven music man

As the pressure around him grew and grew, Rob's innate modesty and self-deprecatory humour managed to keep him grounded, but there was another facet to him which also helped him deal with the stress. This was his love of music: the great passion in his life.

Rob has always been musical; indeed, considered music as a career at one point. He has been playing instruments ever since he was a small child. The role of Edward Cullen has almost certainly set him up for a long and distinguished career, but had he gone down the other route of art-house films, and had that career drawn to a premature close, then he had other options. He could always return to what he originally wanted to do.

He has never made any secret of this ambition, although he has often appeared abashed at the idea of using the success of *Twilight* to carve out a career in music on the side. Asked by TheImproper.com what he would have done if he hadn't become an actor, the answer was immediate.

'I would've become a pianist,' he said. 'I play three instruments, I sing and I write songs. I always say that if acting is my first love, music would've been my Plan B for becoming famous. That may sound a bit pretentious, but it's true. Music occupies a very important place in my life. I couldn't live without music.'

In actual fact, music had been his Plan A until his acting career came along. That is why he has spoken so often about almost falling into it as a profession: his concentration was always on something else entirely different. 'I play a lot of music,' he told VanityFair.com. 'That's what I wanted to do before the acting thing accidentally took off – be a musician. All my best friends are musicians and they have all got their albums and deals, and now I am acting.'

It's no surprise he feels so strongly about it: Rob really has been involved with music all his life. He started learning the piano at a very young age, when he was about three, and between the ages of five and twelve also had lessons in classical guitar. After quite a long gap in his teen years, he returned to it, this time playing the blues, and has continued playing to this day. He has spoken in the past about wanting to be a rapper when he was younger – this, as an example, to MTV News: 'That's what I wanted to do, was to be a rapper. I didn't have the right physicality for it – I'm not very threatening.'

What he really adored, though, was playing acoustic gigs. 'I used to love playing live at open mics at bars,' Rob revealed to TheImproper.com. 'You could go nuts and be completely free.' And it was during one of those sessions on the open mic that 'my first girlfriend's current boyfriend', as Rob put it, heard him, and invited him to join the band Bad Girls.

Rob started to perform intermittently with them, using the name Bobby Dupea (there's a Bobby Dupea page on Facebook now, by the way, although it is run by fans of Rob, rather than Rob himself). Bobby Dupea is the name of the main character in *Five*

Easy Pieces, a film made in 1970 starring Rob's favourite actor, Jack Nicholson, as a former (and very flawed) pianist. This was Rob's way of paying tribute.

Rob later described the Bad Girls experience to an interviewer: 'I was in a band years ago,' he said. 'Not like a proper band, but it had kind of roll-on, roll-off musicians. I liked playing at open mics in bars and stuff because it was the only time I really felt free.'

His family was involved in music as well. Rob's older sister Lizzy is a musician – a singer/songwriter – who often performs with London-based trio Aurora UK alongside guitarist Sacha Collisson, and Simon Greenaway on keyboards. She also sang with Milk & Sugar. Some years before her brother's own compositions went onto the soundtrack of *Twilight*, Lizzy was achieving some measure of success: in 2002, Aurora released a single and an album, both entitled 'Dreaming' and both of which made the charts.

They followed up these releases with a second single, 'The Day It Rained Forever': like 'Dreaming', it got into the Top Twenty. Meanwhile 'Let the Sunshine In', which Lizzie recorded with Milk & Sugar, got to the number-one slot on the Billboard Dance Charts in 2004. Nor was Rob the only Pattinson to get onto the soundtrack of *Twilight*, for Lizzy recorded vocals for the Carter Burwell track 'Who Are They?', which plays when Edward enters the school cafeteria.

Rob had thus seen the music industry from within and he knew what a tough life it was. 'I don't think people should look for a contract,' he told Virgin.net, shortly after his first *Harry Potter* outing had been released. 'My sister works so hard to make money and I think it ruins you. I think it's a lot easier to make money in the acting world, not that it's easier but there aren't so many pressures on you. You don't have to be so humble, whereas in the music industry you have to really bow down to a lot of people to get noticed.'

There spoke a young man who had just had his first lucky break: what was actually happening was that Rob's career was beginning to overtake his sister's. Plenty of people who tried and failed to make a success of it in acting would certainly not have thought that this was an easier industry to crack.

Even so, watching how hard his sister had to work had not entirely put him off. It is this industry that he thought he wanted to enter before his acting career took over, not the world of filming at all. 'It's bizarre, but I never really had any aspirations to be an actor when I was young,' he told the *Daily Telegraph* in the run-up to the release of *Twilight*. 'I wanted to play the piano in a bar, to be the old dude with a whisky glass, all dishevelled. I love the piano; they've actually used some of my music in the film.'

They had indeed, as noted elsewhere in this book: the songs were co-written with his friends Marcus Foster, Bobby Long and Sam Bradley. It was very unusual for a young film star to have his own compositions in the soundtrack of a movie. To sing on an OST, yes, perhaps, but something he had actually composed? How had that come about? 'By accident,' Rob told film.com, displaying all the usual modesty that was still intact, despite the ongoing, intensive scrutiny he had now long had to endure.

'I think Nikki [Reed] gave a CD of stuff I'd recorded on my computer to Catherine [Hardwicke]. I'd recorded it years ago. I think Catherine put it into a cut and I didn't even realize what it was at first. It kind of fit really well. I didn't really think about it [as] I didn't know I was going to be on the soundtrack. I wanted to do it [under] another name because I thought it would be distracting ... which it has been. It was probably all a big mistake.

But I like the idea. I think the song fit there ['Let Me Sign' in the ballet studio scene]. I didn't think it sounded like me, so I thought it would just kind of work. I'm not trying to get a music career out of it or anything.'

He was beginning to strike a defensive note. Rob had discovered another downside of fame: that other actors, and people who worked in the industry, could get extremely jealous of another person's success, and attempt to do him or her down by any method available. The clear implication from some quarters was that Rob's music got into the film for reasons other than its intrinsic merit – nonsense, certainly, but it was making him more sensitive than he needed to be.

Stephenie Meyer and Catherine Hardwicke were extremely supportive, calling Rob's musical work 'amazing' at the Comic-Con convention in 2008. Indeed, Catherine was so impressed that when she took over a guest DJ slot on Santa Monica-based radio station KCRW, she chose Rob's number 'Let Me Sign' as one of her five favourite pieces for the show.

'After we made the whole morphing crazy dream sequence [after Bella has been hurt in the ballet studio] we took that on my laptop back into another little studio in the valley, and then Rob literally sang and just played to the image on the screen,' she said of the track. 'And I just watched Rob sing this song, maybe ten different times. Every time it sounded like something almost completely different, because it just came out of him, this kind of raw feeling, and in a way, that was my favourite day that I've had in the last two years, just being there in the studio, and watching music just come out of somebody's body.'

That was quite a tribute. So was the fact that Rob himself was beginning to inspire music in others. Sarah Williams wrote a song called 'She Wants To Be Mrs Robert Pattinson' for her daughter Chariss Amber, a massive Rob fan, and then posted it on one of the numerous tribute sites on the net. For there were now websites specifically dedicated to Rob's music, as well as his acting. His ability to sing made him, if anything, appear even more desirable. Not only was he a dream to look at and a great actor, but he had poetry in his soul, too.

True to form, and possibly to head off any anticipated criticism, Rob was keen to play down his musical achievements with regards to *Twilight*. 'It's just a weird little song,' he said of 'Let Me Sign', unnamed back then. 'It's really random. It comes at a strange point in the movie. It's towards the end of the movie, but it's not Edward-related. There was one cut of the movie [I saw the other day] that had the song.'

Few would agree with the summary 'a weird little song'. 'Let Me Sign' is a deeply emotional track, its lyrics occasionally blurred, almost growled rather than sung, which worked perfectly with the imagery Catherine Hardwicke set it against: the flickering dream montage that accompanies Bella's slide into unconsciousness following James's vicious attack.

As with 'Never Think', Rob's song on the official soundtrack, the musical style gave a clear indication of his artistic influences. For Rob's tastes are not actually strikingly contemporary: he prefers old blues, such as Van Morrison, John Lee Hooker and Elmore James. Both his songs owed a debt to these geniuses who had gone before.

'Never Think', track ten on the OST, begins with the melody being gently picked out on an acoustic guitar. For over a minute, the haunting, bluesy instrumental is given sway. Then Rob's voice croons the opening lyrics, and holds the song till the end. He has a striking singing voice: steeped in emotion and atmosphere, it is in fact reminiscent of that 'old dude with a whisky glass' he evoked as a former aspiration, seeming to suggest both a maturity and sadness beyond Rob's years. There is something almost painful about his delivery, which is powerfully effective.

On the whole, his efforts were very well received – but Rob found that, regrettably, success in one field led him to have to curb his efforts in another. His growing fame meant that one of his favourite pastimes, singing in public, was now quite out of the question. Apart from the risk of being mobbed, there was the unwanted exposure. He couldn't be so relaxed about performing in public anymore, either at an open mic or a semi-formal gig. As he explained to one interviewer, 'I still try and play, but it's weird now since when I'm trying to do it as an actor, it always seems kind of cheesy. I did a couple of gigs in LA and people filmed them and put them on the Internet. It just ruins the whole experience. You're like, "Oh, that wasn't the point." So I stopped.'

Indeed, Rob had not realized that he was being filmed at those gigs, so when the footage was subsequently posted on the Internet, it came as quite a shock. He also received a mauling from some quarters for his singing on the stolen tracks. It was extremely unfair, but it was another of the prices of being a celebrity.

In a rare, rather raw comment that clearly came from the heart, Rob told TheImproper.com exactly what the gigs had meant to him: '[They were] a cathartic experience for me,' he admitted. 'I've lost a huge chunk of my life.'

There remained a faint hope for reclaiming his former lifestyle. Rob revealed: 'I'm going to wait for all this to die down before I start doing live gigs again.' But with at least another two *Twilight* movies still to be released, and no sign of his popularity waning, he might have some years to wait yet.

Of course, *Twilight* was not the only film Rob contributed to musically. He had sung three songs on *How to Be*, written by Joe Hastings and Oliver Irving: 'Chokin' on the Dust, Part 1', 'Chokin' on the Dust, Part 2' and 'Doin' Fine'. Because of Rob's current profile, these tracks have since prompted a great deal of interest from fans.

Oliver Irving, who wrote and directed the film, professed himself to be pleased with the result. 'Music is extremely important throughout the film and was a part of the screenplay right from the start,' he said in a note on the film's website. 'I am very pleased with the soundtrack and everyone's contribution to it – it truly sums up the feeling of the film.'

What with this, Rob's acknowledged contribution to the *Twilight* soundtrack, and his proven musical track record, you might think that he would now feel justified in calling himself a musician. But for all the longevity of music in his life, Rob remained rather charmingly concerned that fans might think he was trying to exploit the opportunity his film career had afforded him – and treat him harshly as a result.

'That's what I was scared about; it looks like I'm trying to get a music career out of it or something,' he told the *Los Angeles Times*. 'I've never really recorded anything. I just played in pubs and stuff – and I really didn't want it to look like I was trying to cash in. I hope it doesn't come across as that. I'm not going to be doing any music videos or anything.'

Of course, it didn't come across like that at all. Nor should Rob have doubted the quality of his musicianship: in a project as important as the *Twilight* franchise, there was no way that Summit would have allowed Rob's songs anywhere near the film, unless they believed they were of a high professional standard – which they were.

At the time of writing, there are no plans for Rob's music to feature in *New Moon*. However, he did hint that there was plenty more to come in the future. 'I'm in talks to do a soundtrack for another movie, composing,' he told Fandango.com. 'I cannot say what it is yet, but I really, really, really want to do it. I don't think I'm going to have anything on *New Moon*, but never say never.' And he revealed to the *Los Angeles Times*: 'Music is my back-up plan if acting fails. I don't want to put all my eggs in one basket.'

As such, an album is not out of the question, even if Rob was worried about seeming to take advantage of the success of *Twilight*. 'I think if I did it, I'd do it under a different name and not promote it,' he hinted to MTV. 'Maybe I could just do it under Edward Cullen, and we'll see what happens. That would be pretty obvious. But, maybe? I probably won't do it for a while. I'm not really interested in having a music career. I don't care if people buy my stuff or not.'

Actually, he would have cared enormously. But, apart from anything else, at that stage in his career there was no time. For as well as wrapping *New Moon*, he was taking on a whole host of other projects.

His admirers, meanwhile, were being gripped by a very different topic. Had Rob at long last found love?

twelve robsessed

The scene was a familiar one. Hordes of screaming girls lined the streets, while the convention centre itself was packed. Some of the biggest names in Hollywood were there, including Johnny Depp ... but just as he had done a year previously, one person stole the show. It was Rob, back at the Comic-Con in San Diego in the summer of 2009, one year on from the appearance that had proved to the world and he himself quite what a huge star he'd become. That star was now burning more brightly still.

There was one big difference, however: although Rob would be taking part in the press conferences and making an appearance in front of the fans, he wouldn't be doing any personal interviews. Such was the intensive interest in his private life, to say nothing of the massive attention now focused on everything he did, that Rob was moving into the elite crowd, also inhabited by the likes of Tom Cruise, Brad Pitt and, closer to home, Johnny Depp, whereby he was no longer required to give any personal confidences away. It is only the biggest celebrities who can get away with not giving personal interviews: Rob was now in that league.

It had been quite a year. Rob had gone from virtual unknown to top of the A list almost overnight: he was on good form, however, laughing and joking with fellow cast members, and playing it all down, as he always did. In a press conference away from the baying crowds, Rob was asked if he'd changed over the previous year: 'I don't know,' he said. 'I'd like to think that I haven't changed that much. Within myself I don't think I've changed. I think I look down a lot. There's something wrong with my neck. No. It's kind of extraordinary. I don't think that any of us expected any of this to happen, especially that it seems to keep building and building, the magnitude of this franchise. Comic-Con really was the eye-opener and it's just kind of gotten bigger and bigger. It's an interesting thing to deal with.'

As for the highs and lows of the past twelve months, and how he lived a normal life – 'I don't know. I still think it's still so young, to me, anyway. I can't really claim anything to be a low. I pretty much live an almost identical life, apart from being recognized. That's not exactly the worst thing in the world. I never do anything normal anyway. I just get other people to do it now.'

Of course, *New Moon* was going to be a very different movie from *Twilight*. Rob/Edward is not actually present throughout much of it: it is Taylor/Jacob who is the focus of attention, especially as he has to accept his destiny to become a werewolf. How Edward's absence was to play with the fans was not yet clear, but Rob was adamant that this was his favourite of the books because it put his character in a totally different light.

'I think my break-up scene was my favourite scene,' he said. 'I mean, hopefully it'll come off as having quite a few more levels than the relationship in *Twilight*. It was interesting. It was like a five-page-long dialogue scene. That didn't happen at all in the first one and it's quite an interesting little moment. It completely bypasses all the supernatural elements of the story, as well, which I found quite interesting.'

That was, in fact, key to Rob's playing of the role: that he didn't see Edward as a vampire per se, but merely as a tortured individual trying to do what is right. The book certainly took the story onto a new level of self-sacrifice: the character of Edward had always had to hold back around Bella because he didn't want to harm her, and now he was forced to give her up altogether. Rob had seen and appreciated that in the book.

'I think that *New Moon* was my favourite book as well, mainly because I like the juxtaposition of all of a sudden people being ... It's such a hyped character, Edward, and there are so many people looking at him like a romantic hero,' he said. 'In *New Moon*, the way that I read it anyway, he's just so humbled. It's a character who's looking at Bella and thinking that he loves something too much – but he can't be around. He deliberately starts breaking up their relationship, which I think is a very relatable thing and is very painful.'

Rob had another take on it, too. It is in *New Moon* that Edward, full of despair at what he wrongly believes to have been Bella's death, decides to kill himself by visiting the ancient vampires in Italy and exposing himself for what he really is by going out in the sun. Bella rescues Edward, rather than vice versa: a neat twist on the notion of romantic hero and one that Rob enjoyed.

'Yeah, in the final fight sequence at the end, Bella ends up saving Edward, as she does in every single one of the books,' he mused. 'So I find it really funny how everyone looks at Edward as the hero and he's been continuously saved by the damsel in distress. I think he really realizes that in *New Moon*. So I always liked *New Moon*.'

It was sensible analysis of the character he was playing, but Rob was attracting a great deal of attention for something else, as well. For a long time now, speculation had been growing about an off-screen romance with Kristen, but at the Comic-Con, the two of them didn't seem to be hanging out much together. Rather, Kristen seemed to be spending her time with Taylor, even giving interviews with him rather than Rob by her side. What was going on? Had they 'broken up'?

What appeared to be happening was actually linked to the narrative of the film: the studio had played a role in all this. Just as Kristen's character Bella is torn between Edward and Jacob, so, the suspicions went, the studio wanted for her to be torn between Taylor and Rob. Rob was the reason an awful lot of people were going to see the film, but he wasn't actually going to be spending a huge amount of time on-screen. That honour went to Taylor, instead.

'Right now, it's all about Taylor and Kristen,' an anonymous source told E! Online. 'People are pushing them together in the media and behind the scenes because the studio knows the whole world is watching all the time. Rob and Kristen? No. Rob's physically almost never in the movie! The relationship between [Taylor and Kristen] is a huge part of the sequel, so fans need to get used to seeing them together. Not Kristen and Rob. That's the way it's going to be.'

That was the way it was going to be in public, of course, but behind the scenes it was a different matter. Everyone who spent any time with Rob and Kristen bore testament to quite how well they got on: 'The chemistry is incredible,' said their *New Moon* co-star Ashley Greene. 'They're just people you can feel like you relate to,' added Melissa Rosenberg, the *New Moon* screenwriter. 'That sets them apart in a lot of ways.' And it was now known that Kristen's relationship with her former boyfriend Michael Angarano was definitely off.

Rob himself had added plenty of fuel to the rumours. 'I definitely had a thing [crush] with Kristen,' he told *Bop* magazine in July 2009. 'Your first impulse is to ask her for her phone number. And then what kind of birth control she's using. I kid!' But then he diluted that by switching the subject to his *Harry Potter* co-star Emma Watson: 'She is really, really cool,' he went on. 'She seems so much older than she really is. I find her quite intimidating. I always find myself trying to impress her. She's very, very clever.' Was he saying he actually fancied Emma? Rob muddied the waters still further: 'I think we all have the right to fall in love several times,' he said. 'I think you can love ten people all at the same time.'

Emma Watson herself added to the speculation, when she first referred to the fact that Rob and Kristen were an item and then denied she'd said any such thing. And certainly, the publicity machine surrounding Rob had an interest in maintaining he was single: as long as there was no obvious girlfriend on his arm, then he remained an object of desire for all the girls who hoped that they might one day hook up with him. That increased his market-ability, which in turn boosted the profits of the films he appeared in – and so on.

There was another *Potter*-related interjection, this time from Harry himself, aka Daniel Radcliffe. Rob had been very graceful about Daniel in the past; now it was time for Daniel to do likewise. There was no mistaking it: his former co-star had jumped over him – jumped over everyone – in the heart-throb stakes, and Daniel conceded as much.

'Rob Pattinson is a sex symbol,' he said to Usmagazine.com at the American premiere of *Harry Potter and the Half-Blood Prince* on 10 July. 'Rob Pattinson is a genuine sexy guy. He's got the height. If girls like short and nerdy, then I'm a sex symbol! I've said probably three words to him in the last three years and that was before *Twilight* all kicked off. But I wish him well. Hopefully, I'll see him at some point. He's bound to turn up at one of these [premieres] at some point.'

Indeed, Daniel, by virtue of his own experiences, was one of the few people who could understand what Rob was going through, at least in terms of the popularity of the films. He made no bones about the fact that he and Rob didn't actually know one another that well, but he did have some insight into where he was at that point. 'I won't pretend we're best mates or knew each other really well, but we really enjoyed working with each other, or at least I enjoyed working with him!' he told a press conference in the run-up to the release of his film. 'He's doing brilliantly, which is fantastic. The thing that is interesting for me is that *Twilight* is the only other franchise that comes close to *Potter* in terms of the mania that surrounds it, the attention that the leads get and just how global it is.'

All of this, however, was superseded by curiosity about what was really going on between Kristen and Rob. Both continued to deny everything: no one else was at all sure they were telling the truth. And what Rob and Kristen could not do was to conceal their body language. They might have been physically apart during Comic-Con, but the duo could scarcely keep their eyes off each other, visually tracking one another round the vast hall. But then that was hardly surprising. They were encountering the curse of many another showbiz couple – work was keeping them apart for extended stretches at a time. Rob had been in New York filming the indie flick *Remember Me* with Pierce Brosnan, while Kristen had been on the other side of the country, where she was playing the part of Joan Jett in *The Runaways*. Comic-Con was the first time they had seen one another in quite a long while.

Indeed, Rob had been having quite a time of it. *Remember Me* was the story of another troubled couple, this one in a relationship tested by a series of family tragedies, in which he played Tyler Roth, still recovering from his brother's suicide. His co-stars were Pierce, who played his father Charles; Emilie de Ravin, who played his girlfriend Ally Craig, who had seen her mother being killed; and Lena Olin as Diane, Tyler's mother. The whole experience must have been a little strange for Pierce: it was not so long ago that he had been one of the world's leading heart-throbs through his role as James Bond, and now the hordes of screaming fans surrounding the set were there to see someone else.

In fact, such was Rob's popularity that his very safety now seemed to be at risk. Because his status had changed so drastically and so suddenly, the film's makers had clearly not realized what could happen whenever Rob was out on the street. One celebrity website, radaronline.com, actually witnessed what happened as matters got completely out of hand. Rob had been inside the Strand bookshop on Broadway, filming, when news of his presence spread.

By the time he emerged from the store, a huge crowd of fans had gathered, forcing him to break into a run down the rainy street as he headed for the film's production offices. However, the crush was so great – with hysterical fans photographing him, asking for autographs, trying to touch him and in one case succeeding in hugging him – that he was forced into the street. He had a very narrow escape: a taxi cab clipped him, but he was unhurt. It was nevertheless a major embarrassment for the film-makers, who were perceived not to have been looking out for their star.

Rob did have bodyguards with him: 'You see what you did: you almost killed him!' one bellowed at the fans, mainly teenage girls. There were three 'heavies' in total, managing – just – to hold the fans back. Rob himself appeared very shocked. Damage limitation swung into action immediately: 'The reports are exaggerated,' said Vivian Mayer, the film production company's spokeswoman. 'It was not caused by his fans. Production continues.'

But it was another sign that Rob simply couldn't lead a normal life anymore. Indeed, filming *Remember Me* was turning into a bit of an ordeal: fans were using Twitter to describe where he was at any given point in the city, which meant they turned up and mobbed him wherever he went.

The fans themselves seemed to realize that matters were getting out of hand. *J-14*, a teenage girls' magazine, launched an online petition to look after his safety. 'We know, we wish we could spend every moment with Rob – and knowing where he is at all times definitely makes it feel that way,' the magazine said. 'But there is a point where it goes too far. Let's all bond together to protect Rob.'

The kind of life Rob was leading these days was summed up by an insider on the film, talking to *People* magazine. 'It's been non-stop busy all day with people trying to get a glimpse of him, and the crowd goes nuts when they do see him,' he said. 'I think he appreci-ates it. He's not one to make a big deal about it. He's a chill guy and quiet so far. I think he finds it a little weird that people are standing outside all day to get a glimpse of him, but grateful.' Gratitude was in order: it was certainly making his bankability plain.

But it could be distressing. Earlier in the year, Rob and the crew had been in Italy filming the Volturi scenes for *New Moon*, where he experienced something similar and equally unnerving. 'It's a really emotional experience when people are screaming at you all the time,' he said to EW.com. 'When I was in Italy, all these people started screaming in this bookshop. Your immediate reaction is you feel like you're going to start crying. It's so not how I thought I would react. When people are pressing loads and loads of energy [on you], you can kind of feel it. It's overwhelming.' It was – but he was having to learn how to cope.

In New York – while not being pushed in front of moving taxis by marauding fans – Rob was having quite a ball. There is possibly no more status-conscious city in the world than the Big Apple, and given how successful Rob had become, New Yorkers were loving having him in their midst. He was spotted in the Bowery Hotel, the Black and White bar and the fashionable club Cabin, enjoying himself with friends: he was, beyond a doubt, one of the most popular players in town.

With Kristen several thousand miles away in LA, gossip about his love life continued, too. Rob was spotted on a beach kissing his co-star Emilie: after the initial excitement died down, it turned out that this was staged for the movie. He was also linked to the actress Camilla Belle – with whom he was once pictured, in one of those six-degrees moments, backstage at the Hollywood Film Festival, at the time he picked up his New Hollywood Award – but, as ever, everyone's lips remained tightly sealed when it came to who was really dating whom. Camilla did go on the record to say that the two of them were only friends, but speculation persisted, nonetheless.

Plaudits continued to flood in. In June, *Vanity Fair* ran a poll asking readers who was the world's most handsome man: Rob won. E! Online organized a survey whereby fans chose the hottest dude of the summer: they had a choice between Rob, Zac Efron,

Channing Tatum and 'Brüno', aka Sacha Baron Cohen; Rob got 60 per cent of the vote. Sacha himself had cottoned on to the Rob phenomenon: in one of the many interviews he gave in character as Brüno, the gay Austrian fashion victim, this one to the *Mirror*, he commented, 'Ich am not single. But if zat Robert Pattinson vas asking zis question, ich vould be sucking on his neck quicker zan you could say, "Dirty vampire."'

Elle.com likened Rob to another famous actor, but this time it was a step up in the A-list stakes from Jude Law: the comparison was with none other than Brad Pitt – who, coincidentally, had also starred in a vampire flick, *Interview with the Vampire*, back in 1994. In the UK, Telegraph.co.uk compiled a list of Britain's top-fifty most eligible bachelors: the only surprise in it was that Rob came in at three, rather than one (he was pipped to the post, as he had been in a previous 'eligible bachelors' chart, by Prince Harry and George Lamb).

Meanwhile, as the premiere of *New Moon* drew closer, the film-makers, well aware that Rob's popularity was such that prolonged absences on his part would not go down well in the film, were keen to set the record straight about it all. No one had missed the fact that he'd turned into a major star, but given the level of attention now focused on him, there was a danger that his perceived absence throughout much of the movie might actually put audiences off. This was quite unlikely, it's true, given that Rob's fans would have turned out to see him in a cameo role, but even so, everyone involved wanted to emphasize that this was as much his film as the last one had been.

And so, even though Edward might not have physically been there all the time, his presence hung over it all. In place of the famous sequences in the book in which Bella hears him talking in her head – and thus places herself in increasingly dangerous situations in order to hear him talk again – Rob would actually appear as a vision on-screen.

'*New Moon* is not about setting up the world, but it has its own set of challenges because *New Moon* is very internal,' explained the screenwriter Melissa Rosenberg. 'There's been a lot of talk about how Edward and the Cullens are not a part of the middle of *New Moon*, but actually they are. Certainly Edward is very much alive in Bella's mind throughout *New Moon* … I think fans will be very satisfied with what we're doing — one, because it's true to the book, and two, because there's more Edward. That can't be bad!'

As the summer wore on, interest in Rob showed no signs of abating. In July, he appeared on the cover of *People* (which raised eyebrows, incidentally, as the mag made Rob its main story and relegated the death of the famous newsman Walter Cronkite to a secondary tale), under the heading: 'His Messy Love Life'. Again, the magazine reiterated that it was Kristen that Rob really wanted: again, all parties involved stayed schtum.

There were also mutterings that Kristen herself had become alarmed by growing rumours of his closeness to Emilie, but no one could stand that up either. Not that all this speculation was upsetting the film-makers of the various projects Rob was involved with – they were beside themselves at all the publicity their star was generating, and all without actually having said a word.

The closest anyone got to the real truth was when *OK!* magazine interviewed Christian Serratos, who plays Bella's school friend Angela Weber in the films. Asked whether Rob had turned into a womanizer over the last year, she replied, 'I don't think so. If anything, he's become more humble and more introverted.' And of the romance with Kristen – 'I truly don't know. I don't know.

There's a possibility. There's a possibility that it's all BS, I just don't know. It's going to be interesting finding out either way.'

And so to the future. It had finally been confirmed, to fans' delight, that all four books in the *Twilight* saga were going to be filmed, and that Rob was going to be in all the movies, which meant that the work had to be shot – and fast. Rob was getting older, but Edward wasn't, so the last films in the series were scheduled back to back. It would be a very tight turnaround: the third film, *Eclipse*, was given a release date just seven months after that of *New Moon*. That second movie might involve some long absences on Edward's part, but fans wouldn't have to wait long till he and Bella were back in each other's arms for good.

Stephenie Meyer, meanwhile, remained as involved as ever, working on set with the actors, and also sanctioning many other *Twilight*-related projects. Towards the end of June, *New Moon: The Complete Illustrated Movie Companion* was made available for pre-order, and just a fortnight after that, Stephenie announced on her blog that Yen Press was working on *Twilight: The Graphic Novel*.

This latter, very visual venture had an interesting dimension as far as Rob was concerned. For while he had become part of the *Twilight* phenomenon, rather than vice versa, it was clear that his involvement had had a major effect on the way the character of Edward (and his appearance) was now perceived. The graphic Edward would be modelled on Rob's own striking looks: the cheekbones, the jawline, the famous hair. In truth, any other approach would have just seemed wrong.

But Rob did have a life and a career outside of *Twilight*, and it was important to him that he maintained that other existence. Some naysayers were already gloomily predicting that because his star had risen so sharply and shined so brightly, it couldn't be maintained: there was a real danger, they said, that he was going to burn out.

In reality, that didn't look very likely. He was extending his range in *Remember Me*, and talking about other projects as well. Like Daniel Radcliffe before him, who temporarily swapped movies for the West End and Broadway a few years back, there are plans for Rob to take to the stage. Indeed, the director David Pugh, who worked with Daniel on the play *Equus*, confirmed to *Variety* that he and Rob would be working together on a project in 2010, the nature of which, at the time of writing, remains a closely guarded secret.

And then there is his music. While it is very unlikely that will overshadow his acting career, it is still an important aspect of Rob's life: his hinterland, and a way of relaxing and getting away from his huge fame. Music has not become the day job, in the way he once thought it might, but it has become a way of remembering normality. It will be needed in the years to come, for there is every indication that Rob is going to become an even bigger star.

Friends and those close to him say that all the fame and adulation hasn't gone to his head; Rob himself, meanwhile, believes that it is Edward who is attracting all the attention, not Rob the actor. He is also aware that tastes can change fast, and that he won't always live under this level of strutiny, which in many ways will come as a relief.

But he is planning for the future, and taking full advantage of the many opportunities that are now open to him. As for his relationship with Kristen ... well, they have the rest of the *Twilight* films to make together. After that, Rob's love life – and his career – lie in the hands of fate.

acknowledgements

Many thanks to my wonderful editor, Kate Gribble, and to Rob himself for being such a great subject.

Virginia Blackburn, 2009

Picture Acknowledgements

Page 1: Mirrorpix (all)

Page 2: © John-Paul Pietrus/Corbis Outline

Page 3: Alpha (top); Tower House School photograph (centre); © Photos 12/Alamy (bottom)

Page 4: © Photos 12/Alamy (top); Dave M. Benett/Getty Images (centre); Rex Features (bottom)

Page 5: ITV/Rex Features (top); © IFC Films/Everett/Rex Features (bottom left); © Regent/Everett/Rex Features (bottom right)

Page 6: Albert Ortega/WireImage/Getty Images (top); Michael Buckner/Getty Images (bottom)

Page 7: Franco S. Origlia/Getty Images

Page 8: Elisabetta A. Villa/WireImage/Getty Images

Page 9: Lester Cohen/WireImage/Getty Images (top); Chris Polk/FilmMagic/GettyImages (centre); Lester Cohen/WireImage/Getty Images (bottom)

Pages 10–11: © Peggy Sirota/Corbis Outline

Page 12: © Everett Collection/Rex Features

Page 13: © Everett Collection/Rex Features (all)

Page 14: Masatoshi Okauchi/Rex Features (top left); Pascal Le Segretain/Getty Images (top right); Gianmarco Maggiolini/ Famous (bottom)

Page 15: Peter Brooker/Rex Features (top); Jeff Kravitz/ FilmMagic/Getty Images (centre); Francois Durand/Getty Images (bottom)

Page 16: Rex Features (top left); © Everett Collection/Rex Features (top right and bottom)

sources

The author conducted her research for this book using a vast range of sources. These listed here were of particular help.

Magazines

Blast

Booklist

Bop

Closer

Company

CosmoGirl

Empire

Entertainment Weekly

ES magazine

Glamour

GQ

Heat

Hello!

J-14

Kirkus Reviews

Life & Style

National Enquirer

Nylon Guys

OK!

People

Publishers Weekly

Random Interview

School Library Journal

Seven

Saturday Night Magazine

Sunday Times Style magazine

Teen People

Time Out

TV Guide

US

USA Today

Newspapers

Chicago Sun-Times

Daily Express

Daily Mail

Daily Mirror

Daily Star

Daily Telegraph

Evening Standard

Examiner

The Guardian

The Independent

The Independent on Sunday

Los Angeles Times

Metro

New York Times

The Observer
The People
Philly Daily News
Providence Journal
The Sun
Sunday Telegraph
The Times
Tulsa World
Washington Post

TV

BBC
MTV News
Newsbeat
Newsround

Websites

www.AccessHollywood.com
www.agirlsworld.com
www.atwilightkiss.com
www.baltimore.metromix.com
www.britmovie.co.uk
www.canmag.com
www.colesmithy.com
www.EW.com
www.Fandango.com
www.FEARnet.com
www.film.com

www.hollywood.com

www.huffingtonpost.com

www.internetreviews.com

www.metromix.com

Pattinson Music

www.stuff.co.nz

www.teenhollywood.com

www.Teenreads.com

www.TheImproper.com

www.TheStage.co.uk

www.trendhunter.com

www.Usmagazine.com

www.VanityFair.com

www.viewlondon.co.uk

www.Virgin.net

With additional acknowledgement to Reuters.

index

(Initials in subentries denote the following: KS Kristen Stewart; RP Robert Pattinson; SM Stephenie Meyer; TL Taylor Lautner.)